Tea Here Now

Relax and Rejuvenate with a *Tea Lifestyle*

Rituals, Remedies, and Meditations

DONNA FELLMAN & LHASHA TIZER

Inner Ocean Publishing, Inc.
Maui, Hawai'i • San Francisco, California

Inner Ocean Publishing, Inc.
P.O. Box 1239
Makawao, Maui, HI 96768-1239
www.innerocean.com

Book design by Laura Beers

Inner Ocean Publishing has elected to print this title on 50% postconsumer recycled paper with the recycled portion processed chlorine free. As a result, for this printing we have saved the following resources:

26 trees
1236 lbs of solid waste
11,215 gallons of water
2,429 lbs of net greenhouse gases
4519 KW hours of electricity

Inner Ocean Publishing is a member of Green Press Initiative, a nonprofit program dedicated to supporting publishers in their efforts to reduce their use of fiber sourced from endangered forests. For more information, visit http://www.greenpressinitiative.org.

PUBLISHER CATALOGING-IN-PUBLICATION DATA

Fellman, Donna.
Tea here now : relax and rejuvenate with a tea lifestyle / Donna Fellman
& Lhasha Tizer—Maui, Hawai'i : Inner Ocean, 2005.
p. ; cm.
ISBN: 1-930722-57-5
ISBN-13: 978-1-930722-57-6
1. Tea. 2. Tea--Health aspects. 3. Tea--Meditations. 4. Cookery
(Tea) I. Tizer, Lhasha. II. Title.
TX817.T3 F45 2005
641.3/372--dc22 0512

Printed in the United States of America
05 06 07 08 09 10 DATA 10 9 8 7 6 5 4 3 2 1

DISTRIBUTED BY PUBLISHER'S GROUP WEST
For information on promotions, bulk purchases, premiums, or educational use, please contact: 866.731.2216
or sales@innerocean.com.

We dedicate this book to all our teachers and mentors, known and unknown, who have devoted their lives to developing tea wisdom, meditation, and mindfulness as a practice and a teaching. We are forever grateful and humbled for what it brings to all of life.

Thank you.

TABLE OF CONTENTS

PREFACE

in one sip of tea   xi

FOREWORD

tea and the spirit by james norwood pratt   xiii

INTRODUCTION

living tea   I

1 · TEA HERE NOW

embracing the spirit of tea   11

2 · TEA'S JOURNEY

from shen nong's cup to ours   21

3 · ART AND SCIENCE

preparing a proper cup of tea   33

4 · HEALTH AND WELLNESS

remedies for every occasion   47

5 · THE JAPANESE TEA CEREMONY
   cultivating harmony, respect, purity,
and tranquility   67

6 · MEDITATION AND CONTEMPLATION
            the path to inner stillness   79

7 · RITUAL AND CEREMONY
   bringing the sacred into everyday life   99

8 · SHARING TEA
         the essence of hospitality   115

9 · DRINKING IT ALL IN
      nature in a teacup   129

· RESOURCES TO LEARN MORE ABOUT TEA

                                           145

· ACKNOWLEDGEMENTS

                                           155

· ABOUT THE AUTHORS

                                           159

"Drink your tea slowly and reverently,
as if it is the axis on which the world earth
revolves—slowly, evenly, without rushing
toward the future. Live the actual moment.
Only this moment is life."

THICH NHAT HANH

When I take my daily pilgrimage to the tea-room to make a cup of tea, I wonder how many other people around the world are doing the same. Though the languages we speak, the food we eat, and the clothes we wear may be worlds apart, the spirit of the tea we drink can bridge the oceans that stand between us and let us share in a common experience.

Reaching for my tea, I hear the chatter of the tea girls in India who rise early each day to pick the tender tea leaves, filling their baskets several times before noon. Arranging a tray with teapot and teacup, measuring tea and water, I follow the careful motions of the Japanese tea master, who chooses and sets his tea ware according to long tradition. Sitting down with a view out the window, I remember the Chinese tea votaries, who praise the prac-tice of appreciating the beauty of nature while sipping tea. Pouring tea, I join women around the world who tend to their gleaming brass samovars or gracefully lift their heirloom silver teapots, which glow softly with age and care. Sitting a moment in stillness and silence, I savor the meditative peace of a Buddhist monk.

I slowly lift the cup of steaming tea to take a sip. I watch the steam float gently and feel its moist warmth against my face. I take a deep breath and smell its aroma. I let go a deep breath and, with it, a portion of tension. I taste the tea. I feel its permeating heat. I relax and settle in even more. I slowly set down the teacup, and sit still for another moment. I understand, as have many others, what is so special in sitting down to drink a cup of tea. In one sip of tea, I share a taste of the beauty and goodness of life with everyone who has ever been nourished and calmed by tea's soothing warmth.

DONNA FELLMAN

Let me tell you a secret. The authors are going
to tell you anyway, but I get to go first because
they invited me to write this foreword. The
secret they are going to impart is this: The
natural world all around us—Mother Nature—
is as alive as you and me.

Our society and our times ascribe life to the
strangest things. For instance, consider how we
speak of the "economy" as "robust" and
"healthy" or else "sluggish" and "weak." The
material universe, however, we dismiss as
"mere" matter existing exclusively for our use
and devoid of any life of its own. Many of us
even deny that animals have feelings or consciousness worth mentioning.

What we need to rediscover our connection
with the natural world, Donna and Lhasha tell
us, is some quiet time with good tea. Before
long we will realize what a genial spirit inhabits
this plant—and all "true" tea comes from the

same plant—for as we sip our tea, its spirit enters us. Tea has certain active ingredients that soothe and relax us at the same time that other ingredients are stimulating and energizing us. It is the only substance in all of nature that can simultaneously excite and calm the human nervous system.

This spirit of relaxed alertness, of wakeful tranquility, is uniquely present in the tea plant, and when we drink tea, it enters us. No matter who you are or where you live or when, drinking tea is one thing sure to make you feel a bit better and more civilized. To account for this fact with no reference to "spirit" in some form or other leaves you with a lot of explaining to do.

Not that explanations matter much, tea would teach us. Far from offering any way to transcend the material world, tea drinking deepens and opens the material world and reveals its inner richness. Tea teaches us that the material world is not lifeless and mundane. What is lifeless and mundane is our habit of reducing the physical world to its surface dimensions and ignoring its depth. Tea wakes us up.

You experience an aroma in all its fleeting fullness for only about the time it takes to cut open a fruit, and then it's gone. Sometimes a tea's jewel-like color in your cup seems to be something you can contemplate forever. Its taste in your mouth can summon memories from childhood or, who knows, maybe before. Depths open up for us.

Tea allows us to see the material world as it really is and shows us that it's no different from the highest spiritual reality. For where else, tea asks, is spirit if not "here now" in this material realm we share with other spirits, bleeding through space and time at every point? As Donna and Lhasha so lovingly show us in this book, there's no better way to appreciate this material realm in all its fullness than to make tea and take tea and be present "here now" with it and with ourselves and one another.

JAMES NORWOOD PRATT

"As tea mind permeates more and more the actions of your daily life, you may find yourself opening the china closet doors with more consciousness of that action at hand, and in a manner which strives for beauty in your movement. With that approach you may one day open those china closet doors to realize that you have opened the doors to the kingdom of heaven."

BROTHER JOSEPH KEENAN

I

Back in February 1999, when we first met to begin the process of creating this book, Lhasha wrote in her notes, "Are we being nourished and fulfilled by how we currently conduct our lives? The need to satiate, the desire for more and more, whether information, food, or pleasure of any kind, is part of feeling incomplete. We are hung up on finding the one thing that will satisfy, yet that thing can never be found through acquisition and hoarding—it remains in the realm of feeling and being, a state to be experienced, and a process of finding ongoing meaning and significance in our daily living. If our current lifestyles do not offer us these things, then what will?" For us, it is *Tea Here Now*, a synthesis of the formal tea traditions of China and Japan known as "The Way of Tea"— meditation practices, nutrition education, and the spirit of hospitality translated and applied to today's American culture. *Tea Here Now* is the twenty-first century's Way of Tea.

Before we welcome you into the experience of tea, though, we want to share our own personal stories of our journey with tea and how it became our way of life.

Donna's Story

"Real" tea drinking began for me much as it did for Buddhist monks. I used it to help me stay alert yet calm during meditation. I'd make a nice cup of tea, take it to a quiet spot, and light a candle to focus on. My intention was to sit cross-legged and to quiet my thoughts as I let my awareness turn inward. Sipping hot tea was something to "do" until I trained my mind, hands, and legs that nothing needed to be done while I sat.

Years later, I participated in a writers' workshop. Every afternoon we took turns preparing and serving tea for one another. We didn't just pass out mugs; we truly served one another. As host, we made sure everyone had cushions or pads to sit cross-legged on. We provided a candle or flowers as a centerpiece, or a nice view to look at. We made the tea and then slowly poured the tea into the cups. We carefully carried the tray around to each individual, offering the tea we had chosen for this day. We sat together in silence as we sipped the tea and enjoyed the ambience. We took our time, settling into ourselves, letting go of the rest of the world. In this time we refocused our attention inward and to the present moment. I loved these afternoon tea rituals—I loved creating new settings, I loved serving and being served. And I loved sipping the tea, slowly and thoughtfully, in the company of others. It was an intimate, shared experience yet deeply personal. As we began our work, we were all sensitized. It was easier to write, to listen, to speak thoughtfully, to get work done. It was ritual; it was practical; it was calming; it was exciting. I was hooked.

Intrigued, I began my pursuit of tea knowledge. From *National Geographic,* I collected pictures of people drinking tea all over the world and read about tea in their lives. I read books about the history and science of tea. I drank up every bit of information I could find about tea as I sat

3

sipping it from the cup. A mutual friend introduced me to Stephanie Klausner, a tea merchant from Denver who ran a small, one-woman business that revolved around tea. She was not only a source of more information about tea, but she also introduced me to teas finer than anything I even knew existed. And she knew how to brew them all to perfection. Over the next several years together, she and I taught class- es about tea.

It was shortly after I met Stephanie that my husband, Aiy'm, and I went to India. In Darjeeling and Nilgiri, two districts where tea is grown and processed, I made arrangements to tour tea plantations and speak with the producers. But I needn't have taken any special measures to find tea— everywhere I went, there it was. When we sat down in a shop to discuss the price of rugs, tea was served first. "Bed tea" arrived early in the morning in our room at the guesthouses, and tea accompanied every meal.

One day, we went hiking in the mountains above Dharamsala, trekking well beyond the last little houses and fields. We had heard that if we went far enough, we would find a tall waterfall spilling into a very beautiful pool, so we kept going. When we finally arrived, we weren't disappoint- ed by the waterfall and pool, but we were surprised at the sight of a small stone-and-wood hut nearby. And we were even more surprised to dis- cover that we could purchase a glass of freshly brewed *chai* to sip as we sat at the edge of the pool, admiring the sight.

When I returned from India, I wanted to learn still more about tea. The following summer I had an opportunity to experience *chanoyu*, the

Japanese tea ceremony. I was profoundly moved by it. I saw in the ceremony a way of being and moving that I wanted to make my own. As I studied and practiced *chanoyu*, I found that what I learned in the tearoom could be applied to my whole life: move mindfully, stay composed no matter what the circumstances, appreciate the beauty of small and ordinary things, remain focused, and offer tea graciously to everyone who enters my door.

Lhasha's Story

As far back as memory will allow, I was intrigued by the so-called Asian mystique. Whenever I sat for long periods of time in my parents' formal living room, my eyes would gaze upon the paired porcelain figurines of an elderly Chinese couple. Their hand-painted faces and clothing triggered my imagination, and I made up stories about their lives; many images came and many images left. My mother had collected an assortment of Oriental treasures from far-off lands: vases from Japan, cups from China, hand-carved tables, prints, and paintings with exotic faces adorned our walls. I was mesmerized. My mother herself added to this fascination; when she "dressed up," her clothing was reminiscent of rare silks with mandarin collars and often featured large floral, peony-like motifs. Everyone thought she looked Asian, with her high cheekbones, olive skin, and long, blue-black hair piled on her head in twists and buns.

5

I was barely six years old when we first visited Manhattan's Chinatown. The novel array of tiny shops with strange foods like ducks hanging by their feet in the window amazed me, as did the splendidly vibrant clothing stores, the old cobblestone pavement, the teeming throngs of busy people in the street selling their wares, and the unusual sounds of the language being spoken. No doubt about it: I was drawn in. We stopped for lunch at a restaurant whose facade was a brightly painted pagoda, two stories high, bustling with luncheon customers. The tables were set with starched white tablecloths, silverware, chopsticks, and heavy white china cups and bowls. Before I knew it, the hot wonton soup was in front of me, along with the steaming pot of oolong tea. My dad immediately went for the teapot, pouring a hefty stream of sugar from the glass dispenser. As I carefully sipped the tea from the little cup, I knew that Dad had made it just right. The rich amber hue, and the full yet delicate aroma and flavor were things I would not soon forget.

Later, in my teens, the allure of Eastern culture drew me again, as I came face to face with the black bust of a Buddha mounted high on the wall of my friend Ilene's home. In the time warp of several minutes I was touched by the soul of a being so deep it seemed to have no ending. The ephemeral gaze of the eyes; the strong, sturdy cut of the nose; the warm satisfaction of the curved lips at peace in their elusive smile—all impressed me deeply. These were the outer reflections of an exceptional being. I knew then that this was a presence I wanted to have in my life.

Meditation, and then ritual tea drinking, soon became cornerstones on my life's path. At age twenty-five, while visiting a national park in the rugged mountains of California, I embarked on what was to become a morning ritual for the rest of my life. There, among giant cedar, cypress, and sequoia trees, I sat atop huge granite boulders that overlooked the cascading waters below and drank loose-leaf herbal teas, which helped me slowly wake up to the day—and open up to the lessons of a lifetime.

Since then, having a family and raising children have sustained me, and also taught me the necessity of taking a break from my busy life. In the midst of it all, tea time has become my way to regroup, renew, and refresh at midday. Whenever possible, finding time to break away to meditate and drink tea has helped me bear the stress and strain of daily obligations.

7

Slowly and surely, my professional life became an expression of my personal choices, a journey with tea and meditation. I developed a Wellness Practice, counseling and instructing others in healthy living. Tea ceremony became a part of this, and before I knew it, I was introducing women in my classes to this vital ritual. After I moved to Tucson in 1995, I developed a series of seminars on tea awareness and meditation and began to offer them through the University of Arizona and independently.

It was in 1996 that I first experienced *chanoyu* in a special summer class in Boulder, Colorado. Impressed immediately by the aura of this highly focused, meditative ceremony, I was both lured and challenged by its exactitude and artful beauty. I visited a new Japanese teahouse in Phoenix to attend one of the "public teas." It was then that I met my first tea teacher. Japanese tea ceremony would become a profound instructor about life.

Tea Here Now

During the several years it took us to write this book, we found that expressing the almost ineffable experiences we had with tea required a lot of patience. But writing became a favorite time to allow for the tea aesthetic to enter our life as we each sat down lovingly with a cup of tea beside us. We planned writing retreats in Tucson, Boulder, and some natural settings between our homes in order to share what we had written, to critique each other's writing, and to edit and blend the pieces together. But no matter where we met, every meeting was a special occasion. Writing about the experience of tea—the ritual, the ceremony, as a contemplative approach to life and to nature—we infused ourselves with the spirit of tea. We brewed up experiences for ourselves that would deepen our understanding and knowledge of this magical elixir. The process of sharing ceremony, digging deeper, meditating, and exploring new teas and new ways to serve them was profound and enriching. We were birthing a new tea wisdom.

Tea Is Our Bodhisattva

In the Buddhist tradition, a bodhisattva is an enlightened being who is worthy of a peaceful existence in the paradise of nirvana, but who compassionately chooses to stay on earth to help others become enlightened as well. A potent elixir made of nature itself, tea has been our bodhisattva, a spirit that's free to enter the realm of liberation but that remains steadfastly earthbound to guide us through life, and toward enlightenment. The spirit of tea continues to inspire and sustain us with its ancient, enduring wisdom as we face the day-to-day demands of life in the twenty-first century. We find it easier to choose to turn off the television, not answer the phone, sit down alone or with a friend, and take a deep breath when a cup of tea is beckoning us with its fragrant aroma and relaxing warmth.

In his book *Creating True Peace*, Thich Nhat Hanh talks about the need to make time to live. He wistfully recalls how people in Vietnam used to take a small boat out onto a pond. Carefully, they would place a small amount of tea leaves into the blossoms of the lotus. With darkness, the lotus flowers would close their petals around the tea leaves, perfuming them throughout the night. In the morning, the lotus flowers would open as the sun rose, and the tea drinkers would go back out in their boats with everything they needed. They took a stove and teapot, teacups, fresh water, and, most importantly, their friends. In the beauty of the morning's light, they would harvest the tea leaves, make their lotus-fragranced tea, and drink it while sitting in the boat still floating on the pond.

The poignancy of the beautiful picture of the lotus pond and its tea drinkers lies in the wanting it stirs in our hearts. We all desire to have the time for living. Drinking tea can teach us to take the time to live, to breathe, to share with others, and to stop and sit still long enough to feel our hearts and our aliveness. Tea is our bodhisattva.

Living Tea: Tea as a Lifestyle

We have both made conscious choices again and again to live in a way that reflects and embodies the timeless wisdom that is synonymous with the spirit of tea. For all of us living today, the choice to maintain and nurture some quiet, calm, and balance in the midst of a full and busy life requires willingness and commitment. The effort asks of us no less than a daily renewal of our intentions and no more than remembering what is most important to us. Just as in meditation practice, where we refocus our attention when the mind wanders away and we keep coming back to the here and now, this effort becomes a way of being. So, too, in living tea we remain present with what has now become part of our nature, the daily rituals of preparing and pausing, experiencing and doing, and reflecting and gathering.

> "Its liquor is like the sweetest
> dew from heaven."
>
> Lu Yu

Tea Here Now

embracing the spirit of tea

1

"In the world of tea each movement in the making of tea has nobility and meaningfulness. The mundane, trivial acts of setting a fire, boiling some water, and making a bowl of tea are lifted to the level of an art form. . . . In the way of tea this type of transformation is not restricted just to the making or serving of tea, but it can spill over into all of one's daily actions and transform the entire day."

BROTHER JOSEPH KEENAN

How many processes in life invite us to pause, look within and around, enjoy, and give thanks? Tea has been the occasion for celebrating marriage, for honoring the aging process, for acknowledging the changing of the seasons, and for joining in fellowship and peace. Enjoying tea is one of these ordinary and yet extraordinary activities that everyone can participate in. Whether it is experienced formally, as in the Japanese tea ceremony, *chanoyu,* or informally, when a friend drops over unannounced, tea is a way to share one's time, thoughts, and heart with another person.

What are your experiences with tea? Warm memories from childhood of tea time shared with a grandparent or an aunt, quiet times at home on a wintry night, a relieving break from a hard day's work, cooling off a hot summer afternoon with ice-cold tea, or simply the memorable occasions with friends glad to be together and share life? Whatever it is that draws us to tea, we can acknowledge that tea is a remarkable vehicle for bringing balance and wholeness, ritual and ceremony into our lives.

Cultivating the Tea Lifestyle

Everything about tea inspires careful attention, from the methods of cultivation to the moment when we inhale the "breath of tea," with its unique and exotic aroma. As health practitioners and daily tea drinkers, we know how tea has benefited and improved our own lives. We feel we are missing something when we don't stop for our everyday ritual of tea drinking. We miss both the simple earthiness and grounding that the vegetative tea drink bestows on us and the simple connection to the natural five elements of life that are found in tea: water (to make the tea), fire (heat), air (wind that feeds fire), earth (leaf), and metal (pot). The tea experience offers a harmonious balance of forces in an immediate way that brings a quality to life we don't want to do without.

Why tea here now? Tea embodies solitude and time for quieting the mind; a time for slowness, introspection, and contemplation; a time to look within and get to know oneself and one's world; a time for remembering all of the Zen monks, Taoist sages, and tea masters who have guided our way to "being" rather then "doing."

Tea encapsulates hospitality, sociability, and the opening of our hearts and homes to share a cup of tea with a friend or an unexpected guest. Tea relaxes us and loosens our tongue, allowing our natural generosity and good nature to come forth.

Finally, tea symbolizes sensitivity, inviting us to become aware of all our senses. It draws us in to notice its aroma, the sounds and touch of water, and the magnificent color of its liquor. As we learn to awaken our senses and to understand the spirit of tea at its essence, we can fully experience the wholeness and interconnectedness of all life.

The Spirit of Tea

In the teapot, something close to alchemy happens—like the fanciful being in Aladdin's lamp, an enigmatic tea genie is born in a watery infusion and dances before our eyes. The spirit of tea would likely be described very differently by different people. It is culture in a teacup, a manifestation of the spirit, lifestyle, folk habits, temperament, and customs of each unique culture that developed a tea tradition. It is the teacup or bowl itself, an appreciation of beauty in many forms, an evolution of vessels that best express the grace, lightness, and delicacy of the beverage.

14

Tea is an infusion of heated water poured over delicate leaves and left to steep until the leaves release the fragrance, color, and flavor of their essential oils, polyphenols, and nutritive components. When we drink tea, we are savoring a new medium—the essence of the water and the leaves, a liquid both different and greater.

Metaphorically speaking, tea is also an infusion we can take into life. Through the ritual of tea drinking, we can be instilled with qualities that soak us with their essential flavor and leave us with an expanded sense of ourselves. What is worthwhile to infuse? Through tea awareness, we begin to learn the fine art of discrimination. Some experiences are useful and beneficial, and others are useless and even potentially toxic (much like the waste products our bodies regularly eliminate). Through tea drinking, we can use our senses to tell us what to keep and what to let go of. We check in with ourselves to see how we feel before we take our tea and then after. We use our energy level as a yardstick to measure the derived benefit and ask ourselves, "Do we have more or less energy from the tea-drinking experience?" Having more energy might translate as feeling calmer, more alert, clear-headed, and sensitive. A loss or deficit might appear as tiredness, fatigue, weakness, or depression. If you sense you have more energy, especially if this is an experience that repeats itself, then this is a state worth infusing. If you lose energy, then this is an experience to avoid or limit.

Once we know what essential qualities are worth infusing, then we regard them with tenderness and delicateness. Here we metaphorically chew and swallow our experience, breaking it down like a food and absorbing it into our bloodstream of our being. When we assimilate this experience, it becomes a part of us, we merge with it, and it merges with us. Now this quality is ours, and we have ownership of it. Then comes the last part of the infusion process, manifesting what we own.

Manifesting Tea

Manifesting means bringing these qualities into everyday life and sharing them with others—for example, transferring the calm you feel after taking a break for tea and putting it into the stress of a difficult decision-making process at work, which will in turn enable you to offer peaceful, thoughtful insights and creative solutions. It means drawing

15

on the sensitivity you derive from the tea aesthetic and listening with awareness to your spouse and children when you return home from a long day at work. It means using the respect you learned from kneeling and bowing in the tearoom to recycle, reuse, and be mindful of the earth's resources. It means being inspired by the hospitality experience of the tea ceremony to give some of your time and energy to another.

Making Tea as a Metaphor for Life

When we endeavor to master the art of making a proper cup of tea, or anything else, we find that what we really master is our own self. The tea, the water, and the teapot remain essentially the same. But we change: Patience replaces frustration and anxiety. Confidence grows, and awkwardness dissolves. We become calm and centered. Cup after cup, day after day—practice, as they say, makes perfect. If we can apply ourselves and succeed in making a proper cup of tea, then we can take that knowledge and use it to cook a meal, plant a garden, play an instrument, or ride a horse. What part of our life wouldn't be improved by using the mastery of our self that we've gained by learning to make a wonderful cup of tea?

As we develop an appreciation for a good cup of tea, we cultivate a taste for quality and authenticity that expands beyond our taste for tea. For whatever we master in one area of our lives can be transferred to another area. As we make a good cup of tea, we learn much more than technique; we gain an essential understanding of how to approach anything we do.

Sen no Rikyu (1522–1591) was a Japanese tea master who is today regarded as the patriarch of *chanoyu*. One day, one of his students asked him the secret to making tea. Rikyu replied, "In the summer, impart a sense of deep coolness, in winter, a feeling of warmth; lay the charcoal so that it heats the water, prepare the tea so that it is pleasing—these are the secrets."

This sounded too simple to the student. He wanted Rikyu to reveal a hidden mystery, deep secret teachings, and the unknown. The student exclaimed, "That's no secret. Anyone can do that."

17

"If you can do that, then I will be your student," Rikyu replied.

The secret of mastery comes from developing the capacity within ourselves to do even one simple thing so completely that we glean wisdom from that process that is applicable to all areas of our life. If we approach making our humble cup of tea as a means to live consciously, then making a cup of tea can be instrumental in having and becoming what we desire most. Through this one simple act, we can influence the outcome of a day and effect the unfolding of our own destiny.

⌀ When to Drink Tea

- In idle moments
- When bored with poetry
- Thoughts confused
- Beating time to songs
- When the music stops
- Living in seclusion
- Enjoying scholarly pastimes
- Conversing late at night
- Studying on a sunny day
- In the bridal chamber
- Detaining favored guests
- Playing host to scholars or pretty girls
- Visiting friends returned from far away
- In perfect weather
- When skies are overcast
- Watching boats glide past on the canal
- Midst trees and bamboos
- When flowers bud and birds chatter

· On hot days by a lotus pond

· Burning incense in the courtyard

· After tipsy guests have left

· When the youngsters have gone out

· On visits to secluded temples

· When viewing springs and scenic rocks

Hsu Tze-Shu, Ch'a Shu

19

"Tea is a divine herb. Profits are ample if one plants it. The spirits are purified if one drinks it. . . . Truly it is a necessity in the daily life of men and an asset for the fiscal prosperity of the commonwealth."

XU GUANGQI (1562–1633)
Book of Agricultural Administration

21

Tea has been, and is, many things to many people. It was drunk by the ancient Chinese sages to increase longevity, it was communally shared by Zen monks to honor Buddha and maintain alertness in meditation, it was sipped by Asian royalty to promote health, and it was incorporated in contests testing memory and concentration. What began as the drink of royalty came to be considered a necessity for people from all walks of life. It is a way to socialize, to take a break from work, or to retreat in reverie. Legends and stories about tea's origins and value to humankind have been handed down throughout the years.

Tea in China

Though botanists claim that the tea plant is indigenous to several countries, it was without question the Chinese who were the first to drink and value its extraordinary qualities. More than five thousand years ago, the Chinese Emperor Shen Nong, also known as the Divine Cultivator and the father of Chinese herbalism, purportedly took his first sip. "Tea gives one vigor of body, continuity of mind, and determination of purpose," he discovered, and he used tea as an antidote to the toxins he ingested during the process of tasting and cataloguing all of China's medicinal plants. The first reference to the cultivation of tea appeared in 350, in an updated edition of the *Erh Ya*, a Chinese dictionary. This entry explained that a beverage was made by boiling the leaves and was used as a cure for digestive and nervous disorders, and as a salve to help rheumatic pain.

As Taoism emerged in China, it focused on the development of recipes that would create a magic elixir of immortality. Tea was often used in these formulas, and although it had been an powerful antidote for the Divine Cultivator, it was not able to counteract the poisonous qualities of mercury and lead that were often mixed with it. However, it was at this point that tea became recognized for its ability to energize and balance mind and body.

The Tao was seen in everything: a way of life, it connected all things. Chuang Tzu, Taoist poet and philosopher, when asked about the Tao, said there is nowhere that the Tao is not. The Taoist's life was about appreciating, living, cultivating, and celebrating this energy, which connects us all. Tea became a source for this celebration, one of the means toward a masterful and energetic life.

23

The taking of tea in a contemplative fashion, quietly and in a relaxed manner amid beautiful surroundings, has been an important ritual ever since Emperor Shen Nong took his first sip in his palatial herb garden. During the Tang Dynasty in China (618–907), tea drinking came into favor with the royal families and upper classes, who preferred to enjoy their new pastime out of doors, while listening to harmonious music, composing poetry, and painting beautiful landscapes. Separated from the regular tasks and work of daily living, the ritual of tea lent itself to aesthetic and scholarly pursuits. It was an endeavor of being, a time for introspection. Amid this aura of "tea high," poets and tea votaries such as Lu Tung wrote their prolific praise of tea and its wondrous effects. *The Classic of Tea* by Lu Yu, published in 780, came to be regarded as the definitive volume on all aspects of tea, and Lu Yu soon became the patron saint of tea, revered and celebrated for his knowledge of all things "tea."

Renowned for his care and precision in the making and serving of tea, this new master of tea became a favorite of the nobility, frequently invited to grace their table with his presence. During the Tang Dynasty, when Lu Yu lived, water filtration systems did not exist, and the high-quality water necessary for good-tasting tea was difficult to find. Legend says that when Lu Yu was traveling down the famous Yangtze River, he was invited to tea by a high-ranking dignitary. The dignitary ordered his chief ranking officer to go to the river at Nanling, which was said to have the "finest water under heaven," and draw some for tea. When Lu Yu arrived, he took a sip, then put down the ladle in a disgruntled manner, saying that the water was too low-grade and must have been drawn from a spot close to the riverbank, where it could be polluted and stagnant. The officer protested, "A hundred witnesses can testify that I drew this water from midstream." Then Lu Yu took a second sip and replied, "Well, maybe it is Nanling mainstream water, but it has been heavily diluted with water from the riverbank." The officer was in awe of Lu Yu's perception and accuracy. He insisted that he had indeed obtained the water from midstream, but admitted that upon disembarking, some water had spilled out of the container, and he had topped it off with water from the riverbank. "Ah, Master Lu!" he exclaimed. "You are clearly an immortal!"

From tea aficionados like Lu Yu, we learn the art of discernment. This story helps us to realize that human beings can develop a highly refined ability to distinguish the subtle tastes, aromas, sounds, and sights that we rarely experience in our own lives. Lu Yu is emblematic of the expert in us all, just waiting for an opportunity to awaken. He represents the researcher and the scientist within us who thrives on discovery and aspires to excel.

The sixth century monastic tradition of tea drinking in China was born out of Zen Buddhist monk Bodhidharma's resolute efforts to stay awake during long hours of meditation. Legend tells us that he was so determined and persistent to this end that in a frenzy of frustration he tore off his eyelids and threw them to the ground so that he would never fall asleep again. From these two eyelids, tea plants grew. When the plants matured, he picked the leaves, brewed them, and discovered that tea drinking supported the rigors of long hours of meditation practice by sustaining wakefulness. He then taught his disciples the beneficial uses of tea in their daily ritual practices. A new relationship was created, and tea became the friend of meditation.

Tea in Japan

As an honored guest of a high official, Lu Yu might have served tea to a member of a delegation visiting from Japan. Until about the year 900, the Chinese received many kinds of delegations from Japan, including Buddhist monks who came to monasteries to study. For example, in Japan Emperor Saga, visiting a temple to worship Buddha in 815, was served tea by the head abbot. Thereafter, during the historical period known as the Heian era (794–1185), the popularity of tea drinking spread to the upper classes. For them, the taste of tea was exotic, regal, and Chinese—that is to say, highly revered. But it remained an expensive item, rarely attainable. Yet the recognition of tea's health benefits ultimately ensured tea's widespread popularity and acceptance in Japan, just as it had done in China, and would later do in Europe and America.

So far as we know, one of the earliest Japanese texts explicitly prescribing the use of tea as a medicine was written by a monk who had returned from studying Buddhism in China. This monk, Eisai (1141–1215), was the founder of the Rinzai sect of Zen Buddhism in Japan. So impressed was he with the effects of Chinese tea that he brought tea seeds to Japan and enthusiastically cultivated them. He did much for the promotion of tea when he prescribed tea to a very influential shogun who had taken ill. Some accounts claim that the shogun believed he was dangerously ill, though in truth he was only suffering from a royal hangover. Greatly pleased with the relief tea gave, the shogun became a dedicated tea drinker.

Buddhism, Confucianism, and Taoism were all strong influences in Eisai's life; much of his writings reflect these views. Since Heaven has given us life, he maintained, it is our responsibility to preserve our health and maximize the span of our years. But in his day and age he saw very little in the cultural mores that promoted leading the balanced life necessary to both honor the body and preserve its health. Many of his countrymen, he felt, lacked a fundamental knowledge about how best to maintain health. The book he wrote in 1214, *Preservation of Health Through Drinking Tea*, was a medical text expounding the mental and physical benefits of tea drinking. Following his example, priests, warriors, and aristocrats began to enjoy drinking tea. According to a traditional Japanese story, Eisai presented some of his tea seeds to Saint Myoe at Togonoo Temple in Kyoto, where they flourished. Myoe came to be regarded as a patron of *chanoyu* ("The Way of Tea") because of his role in propagating tea in Japan. He is also well known as the author of the *Ten Virtues of Tea*.

In the subsequent historical period in Japan, power was transferred from the long-standing aristocracy to those who strong-armed their way to power. The new leaders emulated the practices of the wealthy to display their newfound authority. At the same time, there was within the Zen priesthood a growing interest and promotion of tea drinking. One such priest credited as a founder of *chanoyu*, Juko (1423–1502), was introduced to tea when he asked a physician to prescribe a medicine to banish the excessive drowsiness that plagued his meditation practice. The doctor explained to him that each of the five organs preferred a taste. Since the heart was prime among the organs, what was needed was the bitter taste of tea to nourish the heart and therby simulate all the organs of the body, eliminating his sleepiness.

In the fifteenth century, the Japanese engaged in the Chinese tea contests that were fashionable at the time, trying to guess where the tea or the water had come from. After a while this practice fell out of favor among certain Buddhist monks. The monks drank tea together in a group, in front of a picture of Bodhidharma. Soon, a much simpler tea ceremony developed, one that was based on Zen ideals and incorporated the influences of the Shinto religion and the Japanese culture. This ritual involved Japanese-made earthen bowls, a simple teahouse with a thatched roof, and floor-style seating on tatami mats, all of which contributed to the development of *chanoyu*. Within the context of Japanese culture, the Zen monks took what was mundane and sanctified it with respect and appreciation.

28

Tea in Europe

In 1610, Dutch traders were the first to bring tea home from China. But it wasn't long before much of Europe was introduced to tea and appreciated it not only for its medicinal properties but also for its energizing qualities. Tea was one of the caffeine-bearing products, along with coffee and chocolate, that were introduced almost simultaneously into European culture. There are those who are convinced that the Industrial Revolution would not have been possible if not for the introduction of caffeine—and the clock. Ironically, many Europeans today look to tea as a time to take a break from their work on the clock.

Many books about the history and legends of tea stop here, because it's not so hard to imagine how tea came to America. But what is interesting to note is that what was true historically in China, Japan, and Europe is still true today in the United States—tea's growth in popularity continues to be driven by an interest in its health benefits.

The Journey toward the Perfect Cup of Tea

Over the centuries many tea lovers have recorded their secrets for making a perfect cup of tea. Emperor Kien Lung (1736–1796) undoubtedly drank the very finest tea available in China. It was delivered to him as tribute tea, a mandatory payment from the tea-producing provinces. Today in China, it is common to see people carrying glass jars with the tea leaves floating in their own infusion. Once that jarful has been drunk, the tea leaves are reinfused throughout the day. The hot water comes from thermoses available within an arm's reach almost everywhere. Even though China produces excellent black teas such as Keemuns and Yunnans, the Chinese rarely drink what they call "red tea." These are the teas that the English came to covet so highly in the seventeenth century. What they call red tea is black tea to the West. It was developed as an export tea, so they drink green tea or oolong.

More often than not to the British, it's only a proper "cuppa" with milk and sugar; the Irish, the English, and the Scottish each have their preferred blends. In most of India, a proper cup of tea is a rich milky

29

brew made from black tea leaves, sweetened with sugar, and sometimes fragrant with spices.

Some of the finest oolongs in the world come from what is now Taiwan, though they often still bear the name of Formosa. In Taiwan and some parts of China, infusions are brewed from the same leaves in several rounds and served in tiny cups. Japan's Senchas and Gyokuro leaf teas are light, vegetal brews, in contrast to the tea served in the Japanese tea ceremony, which is a thick, frothy bowl of powdered green tea with an earthy flavor. Tibetans churn their tea with fermented yak butter, salt, and roasted barley not only to quench their thirst but also to supplement their diet with nutrients.

30

In years past, Russians came to love the flavors of camel dust and campfire smoke that permeated their tea on its way to Moscow from the Chinese border. Today they brew a strong tea concentrate, diluting it with water kept hot in a samovar. Persians sometimes flavor their tea with rose jam. We have a friend who remembers seeing her grandfather from Eastern Europe drink black tea through a sugar cube he held in his teeth. And in Turkey black tea is served sweetened with sugar in small, tulip-shaped glasses reminiscent of the Ottoman Empire (despite the higher profile of Turkish coffee, tea has been the national drink of Turkey since the days of Ataturk, in the early twentieth century).

Obviously, tea transcends form.

Almost five thousand years have gone by since Shen Nong's first cup of tea. At that point in time, tea was an inspiring new beverage. Today, tea is a drink infused with history throughout the world. Gazing into our cup, we often contemplate all that has conspired to transform Shen Nong's simple discovery into the fragrant brew that we now sip so appreciatively in the twenty-first century.

> "Thank God for tea. What would the world do
>
> without tea? How did it exist? I am glad I
>
> was not born before tea."

> SYDNEY SMITH (1771–1845)
> ENGLISH CLERGYMAN

31

ART AND SCIENCE

preparing a proper cup of tea

"Set a teapot over a slow fire;

Fill it with cold water;

Boil it long enough to turn a lobster red;

Pour it on the quantity of tea in a porcelain
vessel;

Allow it to remain on the leaves until the vapor
evaporates,

Then sip it slowly,

And all your sorrow will follow the vapor."

EMPEROR KIEN LUNG

"Would you like some tea?" As tea lovers, when we hear this invitation, we light up in anticipation of a nice little pot of Keemun, rich and velvety, served on a tray with cups and saucers. Or maybe we'll have a few rounds of Fancy Formosa oolong, poured from a small *yixing* clay pot into even smaller cups, steeped again and again until the complex floral fragrance and flavor have waxed and waned. We might imagine a green tea, a superb Dragonwell in a *guywan* whose lid restrains the large leaves as they float in their own infusion until we drink it down, slowly savoring each sip.

Do these names sound exotic and unfamiliar? Well, we are talking of tea, a world that includes a broad range of possibilities. The word "tea" might refer to a beverage made from any number of brands of tea bags containing not only tea leaves but herbs and flowers, or to a drink made from instant granules, or to a cool refreshment in bottles that contain tea mixed with fruit juice, herbs, or sweeteners.

In this book about tea, we are referring to the *Camellia sinensis* plant, and the infusion made from its leaf. And to be even more correct, we should say it's the beverage made from this leaf. In fact, it is only in the last few hundred years that tea leaves have been soaked in hot water to make a tea beverage. Originally, tea leaves were boiled in water and often consumed with the broth. There was a time when the leaves were processed and pressed into bricks; at tea time, a certain amount was scraped from the brick and boiled in water. Much later the leaves were dried and ground into a powder that was whisked into hot water until a foamy head developed.

Technically, beverages made from herbs are herbal infusions, and those from fruit and flowers are "tisanes." *Camellia sinensis*, the tea plant, is an evergreen shrub related to the flowering camellia. It is indigenous to a region that spans the borders of China and India, and to scattered regions of some other Asian countries, though it is now cultivated in more than thirty countries. Tea is the most popular beverage enjoyed worldwide, second only to water.

Making Your Own Cup of Tea

The final arbiter of a good cup of tea is your own personal taste. The universal requirements are time and attention. The essential ingredients are tea and water. The way a cup of tea is made is determined in large part by the leaves that are being brewed. The five types of processed tea leaves that you can buy are white, green, oolong, black, and pu'erh. The type of tea that the leaf will yield is determined by how the leaves are processed. Green tea leaves are allowed to wither and then are steamed or heated and not allowed to oxidize, the chemical process that turns the leaves brown or black. Black teas are allowed to fully oxidize. Oolongs are oxidized anywhere from 8 percent to 85 percent. White tea is sun-dried immediately after picking or taken indoors and heated on a low heat. Pu'erh leaves are truly fermented during the processing.

The particular characteristics of the flavor of the tea depend on such things as the age of the plant, the soil and growing conditions where the tea came from, when it was picked, and how it was processed. Weather conditions determine whether tea leaves can be harvested from a plant just once a year, or year-round. In the Darjeeling area, for example, there are four major pickings (called "flushes") from May to October, and then the plants lie dormant for the winter months. Well-cared-for plants can live and produce for hundreds of years. Good-quality Darjeeling tea may come from plants that are more than one hundred fifty years old. We once had oolong tea from the leaves of a seven hundred-year-old tea tree; the leaves had been handpicked, processed, and carried from China in a shoe box. In the wild it's a tree, and when cultivated it's a bush. Some tea leaves are also picked from wild trees.

The ultimate goal of making a cup of tea is to make tea that is exactly what you like best. The secret of doing this is to be able to repeat your own method time and again. So once you choose your tea, measure it carefully, so that you can first determine how much to use, and then be able to use the same amount consistently. You can use the palm of your hand, a teaspoon, or a special tea scoop. If you have a scale, three grams is a good amount for most teas.

The best water to use is water drawn fresh from the spring in the early dawn hours, preferably from the same area where the tea was grown. Since that method isn't available to most of us, we have to make some other choice. Decisions are very personal, and we are each the ultimate authority on what is the best tea in our own cup. The following recommendations are based on our personal experience and what has been the experience of many tea drinkers we know.

Many people prefer spring water even if it comes to us in a plastic or glass bottle. The minerals add body and can enrich the flavor of teas. Spring water also lacks the chemicals that have been added to the water that flows out of our faucets. Some filters take the minerals as well as the chemicals out. Distilled water is without flavor. Over time you may notice that some types of water taste better to you than others.

37

Once you decide what water to use, heat it up. Black tea likes to steep in water at 205 to 210 degrees Fahrenheit. Green teas give their flavors at about 175 degrees. A fine green tea leaf will taste stewed if brewed too hot. Oolongs prefer to be brewed at temperatures between 180 and 195 degrees. The greener the oolong, the lower the temperature. White teas can be brewed at 185 degrees. You can buy a thermometer, or you can learn to read the water and the steam.

In some Eastern languages, there are words to describe the state of the water at different degrees of temperature, based on the size of the bubbles—"string of pearls," for example, or "fish eyes." Of course, if the water is in a tea kettle, then you can't see the bubbles forming. But you can still learn to read the steam vapor. Wispy wafts happen first, then a slow meander. As the process gathers steam so to speak, the volume of the vapor increases, and it soon emerges as a direct column of steam from the narrow opening of the tea kettle.

The sounds are telling, too, as tea kettles make a lot of different noises before they ever reach the boiling point. Over-boiling water drives out the oxygen and leaves water flat. That will affect the taste of the cup of tea also. It's actually a good experiment to start developing your sensitivity to tasting tea and discerning the effect of water. Make two cups of tea to taste at the same time. Do everything exactly the same, but in one cup, use water that has just come to a boil; in the other, try water that has boiled for five minutes.

One Lump or Two?

Some purists look down on anyone who sweetens her tea and adds milk to it. Our philosophy is that tea is totally a matter of personal taste. You should drink it the way you like it. But there are a couple of things to mention.

Even if you have always drunk your tea with a sweetener, at least get into the habit of tasting it first without. If, in the past, you drank tea that wasn't brewed well or was made with poor-quality leaves, it probably needed a sweetener (or milk) to make it palatable. If you've never had good-quality tea that was well brewed, prepare yourself for something altogether different. If you taste the tea and still want a sweetener, then go ahead. Sugar is the most common traditional sweetener. We recommend avoiding artificial sweeteners, which are made from artificial ingredients. Honey, while natural, can add a lot of its own flavor and overpower the flavor of the tea itself. If you want to avoid calories, some people like the herbal sweetener called stevia. Or be creative. Try black tea poured over a small teaspoon of rose jam; you'll find it exotic and aromatic.

39

As with anything else that people become passionate about, when it comes to tea preparation, there are those who can be adamant about the right way of doing things. Such is the case with brewing in the pot versus the cup. Some like the ritual of making tea in a pot and pouring it into the cup. Others brew tea in the cup with a large infuser. We do both, and can't taste the difference. The distinction, perhaps, lies in the total experience. It feels really different to pour the tea from the pot to the cup. You get to watch the tea, see it fill the cup. There's more of a feeling of ritual and a sense of the expansion of time. But sometimes we may just want a good cup of tea and don't have time to take a full break.

The Agony of the Leaves

To brew a good cup of tea, it's important to make sure that the tea leaves have plenty of room to expand and float in the water. The unfurling process is called the "agony of the leaves." Those perforated balls on a handle or chain don't leave enough room for the leaves to fully agonize and give their flavor. Try to avoid using aluminum. In Japan, some cast-iron teapots come with aluminum infusers, but you should replace these infusers with stainless steel. Aluminum can tarnish the taste of tea, and the acidity will leach the aluminum into the tea you drink—trust us, you don't want to ingest aluminum.

When your attention is divided and you need to be precise, special implements can be of great assistance. Mesh infusers are wonderful for timing the brewing of your tea. This style of tea infuser allows the leaves to be removed at the exact right moment without a mess, still allowing maximum room for the leaves to expand. We have never noticed a diminishment in the flavor or quality of the tea. When you are on the go, a one-cup mesh tea strainer is preferable to a perforated metal tea ball, which inhibits the free flow of the brewing process. Mesh strainers can be packed with tea leaves ahead of time. You can bring them to work and on excursions without too much fuss or bother.

Once the water is heated, you can prepare the pot by preheating it. This way, the leaves can absorb the full impact of the heat of the water in order to release their entire flavor. If the pot is cool when the leaves go

40

in, then the hot water's job will be to heat the pot first, instead of the leaves. In an already hot pot, on the other hand, the water douses the leaf and releases the tea's complete essence; a potent brew is born.

Pouring hot water over the leaves creates the infusion. This is the most sacred moment of the tea preparation. It is at this point that the water and leaf merge to become a new substance, and it is the time when we experience the art and finesse of tea making. We learn to cultivate patience and awareness. The uniting of the different elements is the birth of a third—the tea drink itself. Here the most careful timing and attention to detail are required. No matter what the instructions say about making the tea, remember that they are only guidelines and each batch of tea leaf and water merits its own discretion. The instructions may say to use one rounded teaspoon and steep three to four minutes, but in order to really know when the tea is "done," use your eyes and your sense of smell. The aroma is the most important factor to consider, because the color can be deceptive unless you are very familiar with that variety of tea. As the tea is getting ready, a stronger scent will become apparent, attracting your attention. When the tea is finally ready, there should be a crisp, ripe, and full aroma that awakens your senses. Then you'll know that the tea has "arrived." Now, in this moment of near perfection, your discernment will be put to the test. It's all too easy to leave the infusion process underdone or overdone. If the tea is decanted prematurely, you'll soon be sipping weak, almost tasteless tea. If it is steeped too long, the true flavor turns bitter.

41

As It Begins, So It Will End

We have read about and watched master teachers of spirituality and religion conduct an ordinary day in their lives in an unordinary way. Aside from the fact that they generate enormous amounts of physical, emotional, and mental energy, they also go to great lengths to undertake everything they do with a purposeful intent—they prepare. Preparation is an activity that most of us can be careless about. Even though preparation at first takes time, once mastered it yields more time. It teaches us how to be ready for the real work we do. If you have ever watched anyone doing anything really well, combining both craft and technique, then you probably have seen how they carefully begin whatever they do.

Preparation sets the stage for mastery, which will allow you to repeat your success over and over again. Preparation readies you, and mastery brings the task to completion. Whatever we desire in life, we often need to set goals to carry out our intentions. Then we require a process to bring those goals to fruition. But how we begin our journey has everything to do with how it will end. Preparation is the "chop wood, carry water" of our everyday efforts. It is the daily ritual that makes all the difference.

And Then We Can Make a Proper Cup of Tea

Here are the implements you'll need:

- Good water, either filtered or spring

· A teapot with a steam vent; it can be glazed pottery, porcelain, china, or glassware

- A teacup

· A tea kettle, either enamel, stainless steel, or copper; alternatively, a stainless steel pot for boiling water

- Measuring spoons to measure the proper amount of tea needed

· A tea scoop

- A tea infuser

· A clock or a timer

43

Summary Procedure for Making Tea

1. Heat water.

2. When almost boiling, pour water into teapot and teacup to preheat.

3. When pot and cup are warmed, pour water out.

4. Put a measured amount of tea into a teapot. Use approximately one rounded teaspoon per cup for short-leaf varieties of green, oolong, and black and up to a tablespoon for long-leaf varieties. Remember that tea leaves are variable, so follow your supplier's directions until you know how you like it. For herbal teas, use more and check the recipe.

5. Pour water of the appropriate temperature over the tea leaves and let the infusion steep for two to six minutes depending on the type of tea. Green teas usually brew for two to three minutes, oolongs for four to six minutes, and black teas for four to five minutes. Please check with your tea merchant or supplier for suggested times. Herbal teas usually brew for five to ten minutes depending on the type of herbs. Experiment, and use your sense of smell to tell when the tea is brewed to your liking.

6. Decant the tea into your teacup, sit down, center yourself, and enjoy!

"Tea is naught but this: First you heat the water, then you make the tea. Then you drink it properly. That is all you need to know."

SEN NO RIKYU

"Tea tempers the spirits, calms, and harmonizes the mind; it arouses thought and prevents drowsiness, lightens and refreshes the body, and clears the perceptive faculties."

Lu Yu

48

Our fascination with tea has inspired us to read the works of ancient Chinese and Japanese sages whose wisdom comes to us in prose, poetry, medical treatises, and Buddhist teachings. In ancient Chinese medical documents, tea's bitter flavor is a source of vital energy. According to traditional Chinese medicine, the consumption of tea encourages the heart to pump blood more effectively through the body, the glands to regulate hormones efficiently, the cells to be bathed in nutrients, and the kidneys to eliminate waste products expediently.

Traditional Chinese medicine classifies black tea as a "bitter" flavor and green tea as "bitter with a hint of pungency." The pungent flavor of green tea helps the heart and the lungs to work together, beating and breathing moment to moment. When we breathe fully, we feel refreshed, our brains and cells get more oxygen, and our perceptions become clearer. The pungent flavor also fuels the gastrointestinal tract, assisting the large intestine in excreting waste products. When we let go, we feel unblocked, free, and able to receive life more fully.

Current scientific research validates the tea wisdom of the ancients, as Western medicine begins to investigate tea's potential for fighting disease. As nutritionists, we take a great interest in the latest studies focusing on the health-promoting properties of tea. A number of research papers support the theories that drinking tea:

- Provides powerful antioxidants known to prevent the tissue damage that leads to the formation of cancerous cells

· Supports cardiovascular health by helping to lower cholesterol levels, reduce blood pressure, and decrease the risk of heart attack and stroke

· Helps prevent dental caries and gingivitis

· Helps reduce inflammation in the body, relieving stress

· Lowers and stabilizes blood-sugar levels

· Slows down the aging process in the body

· May produce stronger bones with higher bone-mineral density

· May be protective against developing Parkinson's disease, a debilitating neurological disease

49

· May lessen the likelihood of developing rheumatoid arthritis

· May reduce damage to DNA caused by smoking

· May aid in the prevention of kidney stones

· May help prevent and/or lessen the severity of headaches

The Paradox of Tea

It was a belief in tea's health-giving properties that initially promoted · the widespread use of tea in China and later in Europe and the United

States. But it is another quality of tea—what we call "the energizing lift that also soothes"—which has probably been responsible for tea's growing worldwide popularity. It is so unique, this ability to renew and energize while supporting a calm repose. So what is tea's secret, whereby an infusion of a leaf in hot water can brew up this rare elixir?

One of tea's magical ingredients is L-theanine, a neurologically active amino acid capable of inducing chemical changes in the brain, and found almost exclusively in tea. Approximately thirty minutes after ingestion, L-theanine stimulates production of alpha waves, which can create a feeling of being both alert and deeply relaxed. L-theanine limits nerve-cell activity in those areas of the brain associated with anxiety, reducing feelings of stress. It also promotes the production of serotonin, the hormone essential in creating a sense of well-being and relaxation in mind and body. It is L-theanine that gives tea its specific taste and aroma, engendering the flavors we so much enjoy. When your British grandmother told you to sit down and have a "nice cuppa" because it would make you feel better, she knew what she was talking about.

Caffeine: Friend or Foe?

Caffeine, well-known for its mobilizing effects, can take partial credit for tea's ability to energize. It's been shown to help lift the spirits, but it's not known to calm and relax the mind or body. Caffeine is a member of a family of chemicals compounds called methylxanthines, which are readily available to us in coffee, tea, and chocolate. Caffeine is the only methylxanthine in coffee, while tea contains and delivers two others: theophylline and theobromine.

A stimulant for the central nervous system, caffeine affects the brain and muscles most. Given its capacity to increase mental performance, caffeine can go a long way toward eliminating the stress of repetitive, work-related tasks that can make us bored and diminish our productivity. Theophylline invigorates the heart and respiratory systems, vitalizing the entire body by increasing available oxygen at its core, oxygen which later spreads throughout the system. Theobromine, which is also found in chocolate, does similar things but is present in much smaller amounts.

Not merely stimulants, though, theophylline and theobromine are also muscle relaxants that help to counteract the muscle-exciting effects of caffeine. If you want to sit, write, read, relax, meditate, or spend quiet moments alone or with another, then drink tea.

After extensive international testing, no one has been able to directly link moderate amounts of caffeine to any serious illness. Of course, the operative word here is "moderate." Moderate caffeine intake is considered to be 200 to 250 milligrams per day, about the equivalent of the

51

caffeine in two cups of coffee. If you drink two cups of coffee in the morning, then have a couple of caffeine-containing sodas during the day, and even a chocolate bar or two, your caffeine consumption has veered out of the safe range.

Anything taken in excess can cause an imbalance in the body, with undesirable effects. Many people become caffeine-reliant in an effort to cope with a chronic lack of sleep, a stress-loaded lifestyle, and a non-stop schedule, and drinking large amounts of coffee may indicate that you're living too close to the edge. Also, if you suffer from insomnia, high blood pressure, or an irregular heartbeat, you may need to limit your intake of caffeine. Because caffeine from any source can interact with medical drugs and cause adverse reactions, consult with your medical practitioner about how much tea you can safely drink.

Making the Switch, Coffee to Tea

Many people we talk to want to switch from drinking coffee to drinking tea—some because their doctor told them to and others because they've read so much about the health benefits of tea. Many of those people struggle with the transition, mainly because of two factors. One is the kick that coffee gives. Some people really like it or feel that they need it just to get going every day. The other chief allure of coffee is its taste, with a body and fullness that keeps so many coffee drinkers coming back for more. Either way, we can make some recommendations to ease the wobbly sea change from java to tea.

If you are drinking several cups of coffee a day, start by converting one of those cups to decaf. Then gradually increase the number of decaf cups. Next, start substituting black tea for each cup of decaf coffee. You may still feel that you need your full octane cup of coffee first thing in the morning. Fine, but for the rest of the day drink black tea. Try rich, full-bodied black teas such as Yunnan, Assam, or Pu'ehr.

One of our friends recently said that she thought she was more attached to the half and half that she put in her coffee than the coffee itself. If you are accustomed to putting milk or cream and a sweetener into your coffee, do the same to your tea.

If your goal is to drink green tea, you can use a similar process to adjust; just remember to work your way there gradually. There are so many kinds and grades of loose green teas available, and you can keep experimenting till you find the one you love. One really good green tea to start with is Hojicha, a roasted Japanese green tea with a rich, nutty flavor, more palatable to coffee and black tea drinkers. Lung Ching is a Chinese tea, lighter than Hojicha, and it doesn't get astringent, a characteristic of some green teas that some people don't care for. Be patient with yourself, knowing that it can take time to acquire a taste for green teas.

Decaffeinating Your Own Tea

Decaffeinated teas have been available for many years. Some teas are still decaffeinated by the original method, which involves chemical solvents. This inexpensive but harsh process leaves chemical residues in the tea leaves that are not only detrimental to your health and the environment, but can also alter the taste of the tea. A newer method uses carbon dioxide and pressure, and while it leaves no residues or taste, it's more costly.

Rather than using either of these prepared decaffeinated teas, we recommend decaffeinating your own tea. It's very easy. Caffeine is highly soluble in water and will release into the hot water at a faster rate than the other components of tea. Choose your tea and bring water to the proper temperature. Pour the water over the tea leaves and steep for thirty seconds if you're using green tea, forty-five seconds for oolong, and one minute for black. A large measure of tea's caffeine content will come out in this first brewing. Pour off this initial infusion and now brew your tea for the desired amount of time.

How Much Tea?

Tea may not be a panacea for all ills, as some have claimed throughout history, but without question it is a healthy habit to cultivate. It's one of the few indulgences in life that is truly good for almost everyone. And it tends to be part of a whole diet and daily regimen of people who make healthy choices in their lives. So how much tea do we need to drink? Drinking one cup of tea yields immediate, measurable benefits. You don't have to have been drinking tea all your life to profit from some of what tea has to offer. As a preventative measure, it seems that even one cup a day over a long period of time can have a beneficial effect. But conventional wisdom about how much tea to drink for effective health protection is based on the average daily intake of tea in Asian countries. This adds up to about three cups daily.

Some companies are making tea polyphenols available in capsule form. Is this as good as drinking three cups of tea? Many of the reports we read that extolled the benefits of tea concluded with remarks something to this effect: "However, researchers say more study is needed to determine whether tea should be credited for the health benefits or if tea drinkers tend to live healthy lifestyles." Preliminary studies have indicated that tea drinkers tend to make healthier food choices, are less likely to smoke, and are more likely to be physically active. Specific studies are being done now in Japan and the United States to see if tea drinking is part of an overall healthful lifestyle that promotes longevity. Putting a pill into capsule form is antithetical to the spirit of tea, and certainly not part of a tea lifestyle. Taking time for tea may be as much a part of the healing power as the harmonizing benefits of its chemical constituents.

Drinking tea can become a way of life but not a dependency. It has been shown to strengthen the body, rather than weaken it, and to offer an alternative to stronger stimulants and drugs. Tea supports a lifestyle that is more relaxed, aware, and health-oriented.

What else can we say? Have a cup of tea, it's good for you!

Tea as an Accompaniment to Study

It had been almost twenty years since we graduated with our bachelor's degrees when we began a graduate program in holistic nutrition. Although we had always pursued ongoing education, it was self-paced and informal. We were well aware that going back to school, working part-time, and still following other pursuits in tea meant that we had to improve our study skills and become more efficient and productive. Consistently, what helped us was tea. Tea kept us focused. It relieved mental fatigue and gave us inspiration and motivation. Taking time for tea was something we looked forward to and thoroughly enjoyed while studying.

A concentrated activity, study requires disciplined thought so that we can grasp and retain the written material. Some of its stressful side effects include mental drowsiness and fatigue, neck strain, and bodily tension. Pausing to prepare tea, though, is a remedy for brain strain and disrupts the monotony and tedium that long intervals of mental work can bring on. In the short time it takes to heat some water, prepare a cup, and infuse the tea leaves, you can feel refreshed and revitalized. The rhythmic sounds of the kettle heating, the steam arising from the pot, the fragrant aroma of the tea leaves beckon us to breathe deeper, relax, and reawaken. This is the pause that heals.

It's amazing the clarity that a cup of tea can bring. By simply looking at the brew in the cup, we can see through to the very bottom, as if gazing into a clear lake. We may experience a sense of spaciousness—and what a pleasure to feel this when our heads are jammed with lots of information. Sitting down and taking the cup in our hands, we feel its warmth, perceive its earth-tone colors, and inhale its aroma; we expand our senses and our consciousness, and everything has more room to be. Tea lends itself to sipping for long periods of time. It can be kept warm with tea lights and tea cozies, or you can reheat the water and reinfuse.

For many people, long periods of study are best supported by green and oolong teas rather than black tea. A cup of black tea contains about 60 milligrams of caffeine, while oolong and green tea have about 25 to 40 milligrams and 10 to 20, respectively. Some people are sensitive to the higher caffeine content of black tea. In that case, it is better to be cautious and stick to moderate caffeine doses.

The Energetic Effects of Teas

Green teas have been consumed for thousands of years—first by the ancient Chinese and then by the Zen Buddhists for long sessions of contemplation and meditation when wakefulness was a necessity. Green and oolong teas, which are wonderful for digestion and cardiovascular health, are lower in caffeine than black tea and can be drunk over many hours, usually without any negative side effects. Green tea can even be consumed in the evening without the worry of sleeplessness, unless you are caffeine-sensitive and have difficulty sleeping or are prone to insomnia.

The sweet, floral, woody overtones of oolong tea enhance its wondrous effects on the mind. This tea seems to lift the spirits, raising the energy upwards toward the head, expanding your perceptions and creating more space in your mind. Oolong teas lend themselves to inspirational and ecstatic thought. The aroma and taste impart visions of sweet, fresh forest floors, moist and wet from newly fallen rains. It's easy to picture the place where tea grows: sculpted mountains towering above green lands enshrouded by hanging mists. The visions make it simpler for your mind and body to let go and receive—you are able to take in more information. In China and Taiwan, people drink oolong by pouring numerous infusions over several hours. This process, known as the Chinese Gung Fu Tea Ritual, enables you to remain in one place, stay present, be alert, and enjoy. All you need is hot water, tea leaves, a pot, and a cup. The tea continues to taste delightful with each infusion.

Black teas are rich and deeply satisfying. Brewed with boiling water, they are warming. In teacups all over Europe, Canada, America, India, and beyond, the first beverage of the day is most often black tea with milk and sugar (probably because black teas have the most caffeine). Yet despite caffeine's role as a stimulating drug, many people find black teas to be settling and centering. Perhaps this is because of the clarity and focus that tea brings to our minds.

Choosing Tea to Create a Mood and Sustain Energy

The energetic effects of any one tea upon us may be brilliant or subtle. Bringing our attention to ourselves holistically and noticing tea's effect on our energy can show us how to choose a tea. From the lightest, most delicate teas to the darkest, earthiest teas, knowing the effects of each will help us brew up our own alchemical elixirs.

White Peony

First experienced through the eyes and the nose, White Peony has a distinct appearance in its dry form; its color features shades of silver, gray, brown, and white. Always composed of delicate leaves and buds (sometimes joined by a short stem), the tea looks soft to the eye. The aroma strikes first, a bit like a light, sweet, tender tobacco plant; the brewed infusion is sweeter-smelling than the dry form. White Peony is a light, refreshing brew whose full taste blossoms in the mouth after several sips. Its lingering aftertaste has a sweet residue. It is never bitter, and with longer steeping, a deeper, fuller flavor emerges.

This young white tea has a pale yellow color in the cup and reinfuses very well. Soothing to the body, as well as gently uplifting, it seems to harmonize any disparate tendencies and diminishes nervousness. Drink this cooling tea liberally in hot weather, or when the body is hot for any reason. An enjoyable late-afternoon tea, White Peony offers an easy transition into the evening without being overstimulating. Enhance these positive attributes by drinking this tea in a *guywan* or a glass teacup and appreciating the floating leaves.

Lung Ching (translates as "dragonwell")

Named for the auspicious dragon symbol of ancient China, which represents creativity and prosperity, Dragonwell tea has some legendary origins. One story has it that a dragon was seen near a deep well where the tea plants originated, lending the tea its signature name.

One of China's famous green teas, known as a tea of great balance, Lung Ching has long, pointed, needlelike leaves, and contains a vegetative aroma with a hint of background smokiness in its dry form. It's restful to watch the pale yellow, green, and gray liquor distinguish itself in the cup. Lung Ching is calm, stabilizing, and balancing for the digestive system and the emotions. It's mild, pleasing flavor can help reduce the edge when a restless or bloating sensation arises. Because it's somewhat cooling to the body, this tea is most often enjoyed in spring, summer, and early autumn, but it's best in early spring when the most tender crop is picked. Brew lightly for the best effect in a guywan or a porcelain teapot and cup.

Sencha

Japan's best known green tea, Sencha, is tea for any occasion. The leaves range in color from a mid-green with a touch of yellow to a deep, pine-needle green that tastes smooth and full-bodied. A good Sencha provides a refreshing wake-up call; it's rather like an invigorating ocean breeze, beckoning one to breathe deeply. Its distinct, refined flavor is grassy-sweet with a touch of salty seaweed. Truly a flavor principle in the tea cup, Sencha is an elegant, refined tasting tea, clear and sharp. Drink Sencha to sharpen your senses, stimulate your taste buds, and awaken your energy. It goes wonderfully with Japanese food and desserts, such as moist, rice flour–sweetened bean cakes. The best Senchas come from Uji Province—packed with life force, chlorophyll-rich, and high in antioxidants, they may transport you to a dense forest. To increase the cultural effect, brew Sencha in a *tetsubin*, a traditional Japanese cast-iron teapot, and drink it in stoneware cups.

61

Phoenix Jasmine Pearls

Two pairs of long, tender, fine-quality green tea leaves are twisted and twirled and rolled into a precious pearl. Then the dried green tea pearls are infused with the fragrance of freshly picked jasmine blossoms again and again. Nothing artificial is added—the tropical jasmine blossoms leave their indelible, intoxicating scent to be released with the hot water and steam.

Soft, round, and fragrant—truly, this tea is aromatherapy in a cup. As you inhale the perfume that steams from the cup, notice your face soften, your brow relax, and your smile return. The whole body feels refreshed. While you're sipping the tea, a sense of warm calm can soothe away the rough edges of a stressful day. Ideally, these leaves are brewed in glass so that the gentle unfurling of each pearl is visible. It takes two or three infusions to fully release the gentle flavor of the tea and the calming fragrance of the jasmine.

Jade Pouchong

Pouchongs are a special class of oolongs so lightly oxidized that some people consider them to be green teas. But even their small amount of oxidation (6 percent to 12 percent) introduces the complexity of flavors and inspiring fragrances that are the well-loved qualities of oolongs.

Jade Pouchong is lightly colored liquid jade in a cup, with a fragrance of sweet, soft fruit that refreshes and uplifts. The first taste is reminiscent of tropical flowers—soft and subtle. It will leave a lingering taste of cinnamon and coriander on your palate, and a sweet fragrance on your breath. In order to notice the subtleties, you can't help but slow down and return to your senses. This tea encourages a gradual awakening to the moment, an increased awareness of not just the tea, but all sensations and impressions. Jade Pouchong is a tea for reverie and reading or writing.

It requires attention to brew this tea well. Water too hot for too long stews the leaves and cooks the lovely fragrance and flavor. Water that's too cool, with an infusion too short, never draws out the full floral and spice notes.

63

Silver Tip Oolong

Oolong, which means black dragon, lives up to its name in the long, twisted (and silver-tipped) leaves that comprise this variety, one of our favorites. This tea brews like honey in the cup, releasing a rich, sweet, and peachy aroma. The ever-reliable Silver Tip oolong makes many repeated infusions and offers a delicious drink every time. Complex in taste because of its higher level of oxidation and roasting process, this tea is much less brisk than many black teas and warms the body.

Savoring the taste and enjoying the buoyant effects, Silver Tip can raise the spirits and offer elation. It is too good be an everyday tea, this is truly a mood enhancer for special occasions. Enjoy it alone or with others as a celebration of life's simple treasures. Silver Tip can be served Gung Fu style, with a *guywan,* or in any Asian style teapot that is pleasing. It's is so delightful it could be a dessert drink and a sweet treat anytime.

Tippy Yunnan

The dark, rich color and flavor of this tea reflect the soil of the tropical rain forest that nurtures the tea plants of Yunnan Province, China. But this tea takes its name from its lightly colored leaf tips. Like other dark, black teas, Yunnan's caffeine content is higher than that of oolong and green teas. Look for your mental and visual focus to improve with each sip, as your core energy gets a boost and begins to move, with direction but without urgency.

As is the case with many Chinese teas, the fragrance of Tippy Yunnan has a slight smoky note. Its flavor is full-bodied, strong yet smooth. It is a favorite morning tea for many, as a first cup or to go with breakfast. Many people like to add milk and sugar to the tea, lending a nurturing, comforting quality to the drink.

Pu'ehr

Unique among all teas, Pu'ehr features leaves that are truly fermented during processing—made alive again with microorganisms whose very presence imbues the leaves with special qualities. A potent brew, Pu'ehr has long been recognized by the Chinese for its ability to help digestion and balance chi energy. Pu'ehr brings into balance that which is off-center or askew. If you feel a little off or feel a headache coming on, Pu'erh is perfect.

The aroma of this tea is distinct and captivating to the senses, like the earthy dampness of a forest floor. Take your first sip of this dark, deep brew, and you may start to feel its settling, grounding effects right away. It makes a good after-dinner refreshment to aid digestion or complement a chocolate dessert.

Despite its unique flavor, Pu'erh is quickly becoming a favorite tea in America, and more and more is available. You can buy it in pressed forms or as a loose-leaf tea. The Chinese sometimes keep a pot of Pu'ehr concentrate warming over a candle for hours. To make the tea, pour boiling water over the leaves, using as many leaves and steeping them as long as you like. This tea won't get bitter, and if it gets strong, it can be diluted with hot water to taste. The leaves yield several infusions no matter how they are brewed.

"You can taste and feel, but not describe, the exquisite state of repose produced by tea, that precious drink which drives away the five causes of sorrow."

EMPEROR CHIEN LUNG (1710–1799)

THE JAPANESE TEA CEREMONY
cultivating harmony, respect,
purity, and tranquility

"In the practice of tea, a sanctuary is created
where one can take solace in the tranquility of
the spirit."

SEN SOSHITSU XV

Chanoyu, the Japanese tea ceremony, is a ritual that draws from the wisdom of ancient Taoism, Shintoism, Zen Buddhism, and the Chinese and Japanese cultures. Zen came to Japan from monks who studied in Ch'an, China. Ch'an, or Zen, developed from Taoism. Taoism was based on "The Great Tao," the unnameable, unknowable way. The Japanese tea practitioners adopted this term and aptly called the ceremony "The Way of Tea." The Zen founders of the Japanese tea ceremony that is practiced today drew from their roots the "conception of greatness in the smallest incidents of life," writes Okakura in *The Book of Tea*. It was Zen and the idea of *wabi*, or simplicity in everyday life, that encouraged a conservation of resources, as well as an effort to see the whole universe within any one thing and to experience natural beauty.

In *chanoyu*, the degree of awareness that's applied to every task and movement is not something we typically see in our usual way of doing and thinking. *Chanoyu* teaches us to move slowly, treating every utensil as a prized possession, and helps the body to absorb these movements through artful, focused repetition. When the whisk for whipping the tea into a frothy foam is to be set down on the mat, it is placed just so, as we move from our center with our hands, arms, and even each finger in a certain manner. We breathe, keeping our head straight, allowing our shoulders to be relaxed, and not forgetting that the tea is being made for a special guest. Why is all this being so carefully constructed? There are many reasons.

When asked, every practitioner of *chanoyu* may give a different reason for "doing tea." It could be because this practice develops mindfulness, the ability to focus and stay present, to learn to engage our mind, hands, and heart in a unified purpose. It could be because it helps us to move with grace and intention, or because it offers the opportunity to exercise our mind and body at once. But whatever the reason we come to this practice, it is the way that the practice becomes a part of us beyond the tearoom—a thought here, a gesture there—that keeps us practicing tea.

Once we have made *chanoyu* part of our lives, we begin to notice that there are little things that we do differently, like setting the lid of the cooking pot down on the counter carefully. Or not knocking into the furniture as we vacuum. We may enter a room and pause to notice the surroundings, and we may set our shoes together by the door rather than kick them off in a pile. Where once we were careless, now we are careful; where we were distracted, now we are focused; where we were unaware, now we are sensitive; where we were frantic, now we are calm. Where we once took things for granted, a sense of awe for the simple pleasures at hand fills us with joy. We're not constantly making and drinking tea, but tea consciousness begins to steep into the fiber of our muscles and our being. The way of tea becomes a way of life.

69

Entering the Tearoom

Within the walls of the tearoom, the enveloping atmosphere reminds us to feel, smell, taste, hear, and see beauty in the mundane and the imperfect. The host has anticipated our every need and has made an effort to ensure that the food, the ambience, and the tea itself are pleasing to every sense. The flowers, the kettle, every piece used to serve the food and make the tea, have been chosen to delight the eye and to create a sense of harmony.

Entering the tearoom, we enter another world. Here the absence of furniture and casual decor emphasizes the meaningfulness of everything that is present. There is nothing to distract us from focusing on the beauty and the fullness of the moment. In *chanoyu*, when a guest first enters the tearoom, he or she proceeds to the *tokonomo*, a scroll with mounted calligraphy that's been chosen to subtly impart the theme of the gathering. Or we may see a woven basket containing a single flower poised among some grasses, as they would appear in a field. One at a time, each guest kneels and pauses before *tokonomo*. Taking the time to appreciate each utensil for its special and unique attributes is an important part of the ceremony. Then we proceed to the tatami mat, where the host will sit to prepare the tea. Here again, we kneel and pause, this time to gaze at the cast-iron kettle and any other utensils that will be used today to prepare the tea.

After we have seated ourselves, the host or hostess begins the ceremony. There could be an entire meal, or it could begin with serving sweets. In either case, the food that is offered is a feast for the eyes, as well as the mouth. The tea itself is prepared with carefully choreographed movements reflecting their Zen roots and marked by simplicity, economy of motion, attention to detail, and utilitarianism.

Being served by the host helps create for the attendees an ease with whatever unfolds in each moment. Sitting on tatami mats makes us more attuned to our body and posture. The tea itself—frothy, vibrant green, sharp and grassy-tasting—awakens the eyes, nose, and palate to a world of sensory awareness. The tea ceremony is a symphony for our senses. Each sense is engaged and awakened in the art of tea. The refinement of the senses cultivated in the tearoom is a gift that enriches every aspect of our lives.

71

Sen no Rikyu established certain guidelines for the host and the guest at a tea gathering . The virtues of *wa, kei, sei*, and *jaku*, which are expressed in *chanoyu*, translate as harmony, respect, purity, and tranquility, respectively.

Wa, or harmony, is created by bringing all the elements of the tea ceremony into balance so that distinctions between them begin to disappear. This harmony is reflected in the union between the participants and between the host and guests, in the arrangement of the room, in the foods served, and in the tea implements. Influenced by the season, the occasion, and mood of the day, all of these relationships are in a dynamic balance that is meticulously acknowledged and honored. *Wa* signifies an inner harmony, gentleness of spirit, and the subdued, meditative mood felt in the tearoom. In this way, *chanoyu* recognizes and reenacts a universal harmony that instills a sense of oneness and peace in all present.

Kei, or respect, originates from a deep abiding love for all of nature and other beings. It means allowing each thing and person to be itself; it means approaching all entities as special and complete within themselves, as well as honoring mutual boundaries. Nature allows all things their due. In the tearoom, we show *kei* to all people, objects, things, tea, and food by slowing down, pausing, bowing, and expressing attentive admiration and appreciation. As formal as it may seem to bow even to a scroll and to take the time to admire almost every utensil, we embody *kei* in the tearoom when we are living the wisdom of the natural world and respecting all beings for who they are.

Sei, or purity, is the act of "removing the dust of the world from one's heart and mind," writes Sen Soshito XV. The host anticipates the guests' arrival by cleaning the teahouse and putting things in order in the tearoom and within himself or herself. Sweeping the garden and attending to all the details puts one in a frame of mind of "readiness" without distraction. During the ceremony, the host symbolically purifies the perfectly clean utensils in preparation for the ritual and offers guests the opportunity to mentally cleanse themselves of any "impurities" that would stand as impediments to full participation in the ceremony.

Jaku is tranquility, representing the culmination of the experience of harmony, respect, and purity in the tearoom. *Jaku* also refers to a state of inner peace and freedom. This state of tranquility is not so much a product of finding ourselves in a world made perfect, but of finding perfection in the world-as-it-is. The profound acceptance of whatever is present allows us to embrace all of life. Through *chanoyu* we learn that tea is acceptance of the insufficient and that everything we need is contained in this moment. Each sight, smell, taste, and touch is perfect. The tearoom is a universe in miniature. When we create tranquility in the tearoom, we sow the seeds for becoming tranquil in life.

73

The Flowers in the Field

Flowers in a field all contain their own striking and unique features, but when we find them together as they occur in nature, they appear in harmony. While they're each special, not one is overpowering, or detracting from the enjoyment of the whole. When we host a tea gathering, we want to refrain from drawing any undue attention to ourselves, even though we have a prominent role to play. This is part of the inner teaching of *chanoyu*, which encompasses a spirit of contained generosity, in which we give of ourselves with humility and integrity. In a sense, the host or hostess in *chanoyu* conceals a part of his or her self. What is unrevealed and held in abeyance is the ego. Through tea etiquette, the ego is not allowed to dominate the atmosphere; instead the equality of all people comes to the forefront.

Despite all the established protocols of *chanoyu,* even a *chajin,* a regular practitioner who attends many ceremonies, will tell you that no two are alike. The Japanese have a phrase to capture this phenomenon: "*ichigo-ichie,*" which translates as "one meeting, one time." This saying often appears on a scroll in the tearoom, reminding us of the bittersweet wisdom that in each and every gathering we have a once-in-a-lifetime opportunity to experience this present moment with the entirety of our being. This particular time and space will never again be the same; it is unique and precious. Here we touch the eternal, sacred, ever-changing nature of existence. We taste the paradox of the spirit of tea—its evanescence and its enduring, essential nature.

The essential elements of the Japanese tea ceremony are:

· Changing clothes upon arrival

· Walking through a garden

· Purifying our hands and mouth with water

· The host cleaning all utensils

> · Bowing to demonstrate respect before entering the tearoom

· Handling utensils with great care and admiring its physical beauty

> · Using all the senses attentively

· Participating in cordial and considerate conversation

> · Sitting in silence, experiencing, and enjoying

The Japanese tearoom is a special environment where we experience:

> · The fine attunement of our senses to every sound, sight, taste, smell, and touch

· An environment dedicated to simplicity

> · An attentiveness to what is present

· A mindfulness of movement without distracting mannerisms

> · A valuing of quality over quantity and sincerity over pretentiousness

· A commitment to provide for ourselves and our guests

> · Above all, the harmony, purity, and respect that will result in a feeling of tranquility

Creating Your Own Tearoom

Your own tearoom should be a place where you refine and cleanse your senses. It should be a space that delights and nourishes you, that helps create balance and harmony. In the best tearooms, we find simplicity without austerity, limitation without barrenness. Don't worry about getting it perfect, though—we always reserve for ourselves the freedom to experiment and change our tearoom to match our mood or suit the season.

Designing Your Own Tea Ritual

The wisdom of Eastern tea traditions can be translated into a new tea language and design that means as much to you as *chanoyu*. There are many variations in the complete repertoire of *chanoyu* ceremonies. The forms vary to suit the season and time of day, the environment, the host, and the guests—in short, to suit the situation. As we deepen our practice and study of chanoyu, we learn how important a quality "appropriateness" is—creating tea rituals that bring harmony to our own cultural and personal environment, and to ourselves and others, is appropriate.

Traditional tea ceremonies are to tea what ballet is to a dancer: they are the formal body of knowledge that provides a foundation of techniques and cultivates a taste for quality. Some exposure to traditional arts often gives us a structure in which we can develop; from there, we can go on to discover our personal creativity. As with other arts, when we are developing our own tea ceremony, we do not need to stick to a prescribed form; we can adapt that form to bring forth our hearts' innermost longing.

Your own tea ritual might include:

> · A brief walk outside, where you refresh yourself by breathing deeply and leaving behind other concerns

· A ceremonial purification

> · A short meditation to help you pause, slow down, and center yourself before making the tea

· Formal acknowledgement for what you are doing, such as bowing or saying a prayer

> · The intention to handle all objects with great care, as if each one were a sacred object

· The use of your senses as you prepare the tea, watch carefully, smell freely, taste fully, listen attentively, and touch respectfully

> · A willingness to enjoy all the steps of tea preparation so that you can become absorbed in what you are doing

· A full recognition of each guest's presence

· Time to allow the quiet and peace to permeate your being, and the tea to awaken and relax you at the same time

Sit in an upright position, center yourself, become aware of your breath, close your eyes, be present, settle in, and then begin drinking the tea, as a host or a guest.

"Can we make our day, or part of a day, a Japanese tea ceremony, so that every movement—reaching, bending, turning—becomes a ceremony? When we practice in this way, or even practice practicing like this, then it is encouraging and inspiring to see how powerfully and quickly the awareness and understanding deepen and grow."

JOSEPH GOLDSTEIN
Seeking the Heart of Wisdom

78

MEDITATION AND CONTEMPLATION
the path to inner stillness

❧6❧

"Just a cup of tea. Just another opportunity for
healing. Just the hand reaching out to receive
the handle of the cup. Just noticing hot.
Noticing texture and fragrance. Just a cup of
tea. Just this moment in newness. Just the
hand touching the cup. Just the arm retract-
ing. . . . What a wonderful cup of tea. The tea
of peace, of satisfaction. Drinking a cup of
tea, I stop the war."

STEPHEN LEVINE

Historically and culturally, tea time is about making time to be, taking a break, spending time alone, or opening the heart in hospitality. When we thoughtfully partake of tea and approach it in a contemplative manner, we create the time and space to honor ourselves, each other, and our world.

Developing a contemplative way of life unlocks within us a way of being and seeing that opens the door to the inner dimensions of our experience. The word "contemplation" has at its root the Latin word *temple,* which means "a space marked out," or a sanctuary. This space, whether physically created or experienced in our minds, is a still and sacred place where we can reflect on our world. When we contemplate, we enter our own personal sanctuary, leaving behind the entanglements of our day-to-day life and giving us enough space to view them with perspective.

In the *I Ching,* a wisdom book handed down from the Taoist and Confucian sages, an entire chapter is devoted to the hexagram Contemplation. The ancient Chinese symbol for contemplation was a tower that commanded a wide vista of the surrounding region and gave the ancient rulers a long view of their kingdom, enabling them to govern wisely. From our own tower of contemplation, we also are able to see with clarity what the *I Ching* called contemplation, "the divine meaning underlying the workings of the universe." Here we pause in order to gain some perspective on our own internal kingdom, to observe the subtle, moment-to-moment workings of our lives. Taking our daily cup of tea can be our temple, a time and space set apart to stop and reflect.

The Pure Land

In formal Asian tea practice, the tearoom is meant to be a world of its own, with its own values and sense of time, and its own aesthetic. In *chanoyu*, the tearoom takes some inspiration from the concept of the "pure land" of Buddhism. The pure land is an ideal environment where one's own Buddha nature can be swiftly attained, but to enter, a person must leave the earthly world behind. For us, tea becomes a time to reside in our own pure land, to disentangle ourselves from the demands of the day, if only for a little while. Even if our tearoom is nothing more than a seat on our couch where we gaze into the neighbor's trees, having stopped the day to mindfully prepare and drink our tea, we can begin to sort out our lives through contemplation.

81

Formal Meditation and Tea

Tea pays homage to meditation every time a person slows down and enters the world of sensitivity, aestheticism, and beauty, with the heightened awareness of the moment that comes with tea. The practice of meditation gives tea a special meaning and context as a way to "be" with things. We create a unique space—choose a posture, delineate a time, and focus in a way that is distinct from the rest of our lives. Learning to be with ourselves is a process of coming home. We cast our attention inward as we carve out a niche of time and space where we leave the world behind. We quiet ourselves, learning to rest our attention as we relax, focusing on our body and inner being. During this time, we develop concentration; we slow ourselves down; we breathe, observe, and learn. We learn to witness without judgment, accept what is present, and find the still point within.

Mindfulness and Tea:
Awareness of the Present Moment

An ancient practice derived from the teachings of the Buddha, mindfulness is the practice of bringing our full awareness and presence to the simplest detail of each component of our experience. When we bring this moment-by-moment attention to meditation, our meditation becomes grounded in the body, as well as in our feelings and thought processes—it's a holistic attention to life itself. This fullness of being and perceiving cultivates a fine attunement to ourselves and how we interface with the world. It is the ground through which we see clearly in each moment.

Through the application of present-moment awareness, we begin to see the ways we are unfocused and distracted. We may notice that we spend a great deal of time living in our head, caught in thinking about the future or reliving the past, both of which can be stressful and dissatisfying. Being able to see our present situation clearly awakens us to what is possible and what we can do; it's one of the first steps toward a mindful life. When we learn to refocus our attention on what is here now, distractions will diminish, our thinking will slow down, and clarity can emerge. The process of returning again and again to what is at hand is a gateway to a life lived completely, without unnecessary stress and suffering.

Living mindfully can be likened to placing a magnifying lens on reality. Things we may have been oblivious to, ignored, or taken for granted come into focus. The details of every experience, previously hazy, are now illuminated. We may be walking down a street in our usual "let's get to where we are going" mode, mentally ahead of ourselves. Yet, if we have chosen to be mindful, we begin to walk slowly and see the environment through which we are passing. Looking around, we notice something glistening. We find a simple rock composed of minute quartz crystals. No longer an ordinary rock, it strikes us as a gem. Has the rock changed our ability to see things clearly? Or has our attention become magnified through the application of present-moment awareness? Mindfulness helps us discover these simple acts of awareness, bringing us great joy and satisfaction.

We can bring this heightened state of happiness to the serving and drinking of tea. The tea etiquette—committing our attention to whatever arises and putting the needs of others before our own—makes us more devoted to the moment, less apt to have a wavering mind, and more engaged in the world.

Tea mindfulness also brings us back to our senses. We see with fresh eyes, hear with receptive ears, smell with unbiased nostrils, taste with all the taste buds, and touch without judgment. Relieved of our preconceptions and free to connect with our childlike desire to explore and discover, now we come to the experience of being most alive through tea. We live the "miracle of mindfulness," dwelling in a state of joy, awe, and gratitude where all things are possible.

84

The more mindfully we make our tea, the better it tastes. We slow down enough to savor every aspect of the tea experience and find that we have made a superior cup of tea.

Tea Expresses Buddha Nature

In formal meditation practice, we are granted the opportunity to sit in a posture that embodies the archetype of a Buddha. Few forms capture and transmit the essence of an activity in such an immediate and profound way. Through the reenactment of the Buddha's sitting position, we come closer to experiencing our own Buddha nature. In many ways, this is a shortcut to enlightenment, for we do not have to go through all the trial and error that the Buddha did to find a bodily expression for our own true self.

A tea ceremony—*chanoyu*, in particular—is a practice that expresses this Buddha nature in action. The values of simplicity, humility, respect, purity, and tranquility represent the nature we all have within us. Regrettably, in modern-day life, we may feel estranged from our virtues and capabilities, deprived of this natural fulfillment of our being. A tea ceremony, which brings us back to the here and now, can put us in touch again with our innate capacities, showing us how we can truly be ourselves and lifting us to our highest attributes.

The Zen Buddhist tradition of tea, which replaced the more fanciful and elegant tea drinking of earlier periods, reflects the essence of simplicity. In *The Way of Tea and Buddhism*, Hisamatsu Shin'ichi said, "Tea drinking is in itself the attainment of Buddhahood and the spontaneous activity of an enlightened being." Zen views all of life as part of Buddha nature. According to Saito Yuriko in *The Japanese Gardens*, this means that ". . . a common place, rock or a broken tea bowl is as valuable as a gorgeous painting or an expensive porcelain bowl. Similarly, activities generally regarded as mundane, such as eating and sweeping the ground, are equally as significant as studying Buddhist texts and meditating." The quiet simplicity of Zen was the seed from which *chanoyu* was born. Zen's virtues became part of *chanoyu's* ambience, a calm environment meant to support an unassuming state of mind.

85

Tea and Equanimity: Life in Balance

Since ancient times, drinking tea in a ceremonial manner offered tranquility to a turbulent world. Today, thousands of years later, tea drinking yields the same benefits of sitting quietly in mindfulness and presence. This opens the door to a pure and even heart. The intentional, ritual action of tea drinking still helps to establish equanimity. Equanimity is a state in which one's mind and body remain composed and calm, even in the face of disturbance or adversity. The word "equanimity" derives from the Latin word *aequs*, which means "balanced," and from *animus*, which means "spirit" or "internal state." Equanimity, then, is the achievement of a balanced, internal state.

In *chanoyu*, we learn to accept whatever the situation presents. We make the intentional effort to serve our guests to the best of our ability. If we are playing the role of the host and forget to clean the tea scoop, if we add more water than necessary to the tea, or even if we drop a tea bowl, we carry on, persisting in our efforts, remaining composed. Similarly, when we are guests, we may forget to say thank you or appreciate the tea ware, but we accept our oversight and continue to enjoy each other and the day! This way of being allows us to notice our mistakes without dwelling on them. We refrain from losing our present-moment awareness and drifting into preoccupation. We discover that practicing a tea ritual infuses our being with a centeredness we may not have thought was possible. We gain the skill of remaining calm under pressure. We learn the art of noninterference in the movement of unfolding events, allowing them to be as they are. We observe and live in the flow of life, noticing that all circumstances, feelings, thoughts, and sensations will come and go. Soon we are experiencing a newfound ease in whatever we do.

Tranquility:
Tea Drinking as a Contemplative Experience

The concept of tranquility suggests a gentle coolness, a quality of temperament that can smooth the inner landscape of our being. Like a cooling-off period, during which we separate ourselves from turbulent emotions, tranquility enables us to remain calm and not to react to destructive influences. But how can anyone exist in a tranquil state when we so easily get riled up by circumstances and emotions?

87

When we thoughtfully consider how we approach our daily tasks, like taking time to brew, serve, or drink tea, we can create an environment that invites tranquility. It is all too easy to feel overwhelmed by life these days, but the choice to dedicate precious time and space to tea halts this momentum, providing us with both a refuge from busyness and an opportunity for inner reflection. The wider perspective that this reflection engenders makes us less likely to become emotionally reactive to the ups and downs of everyday life.

Both the accumulation and benefit of all mindfulness practices, tranquility is born out of our devotion to live with awareness day in and out. The continual efforts we make to be with ourselves, to notice our experience, to listen to our bodily sensations, and to ponder our life add up to a small investment of significant magnitude. The simple action of tea drinking says no to getting pulled outside ourselves, and yes to cultivating a deeper inner life. Tranquility is truly a gift to be cherished.

Tea as a Transitional Activity

Transitions provide a link between activities, teaching us how to complete one thing and prepare for the next. Think of transitions as the joints in our bodies: if they are working well, our motion is smooth and continuous; if they are stiff or nonfunctional, we feel tension or pain. When we don't transition with awareness, we can feel cut off, separate, fragmented, incomplete, and unprepared to undertake the next thing in our life without a lot of stress. Transitions help to ready us for whatever we are about to do.

A tea transition helps us to bring the meditative practice into everyday life. During our own tea ritual, we learn to move in slow and mindful ways while making our tea and holding the teacup in our hands as we get up from the meditation cushion. We taste how to preserve mindfulness by being aware of each thing we are doing, not pulled ahead of ourselves, not lapsing into the future. In fact, this is the epitome of the meaning of "Tea Here Now," a practice of living tea in every moment.

Shinzen Young, a Buddhist meditation teacher, calls transitions "gateways of opportunity." When we are in the process of transition, we are in an in-between state, between roles and activities, not really one thing or another. When we partake of tea in a conscious way, we become more fluid, like the tea liquid; more vaporous, like steam; and more ethereal, like the aroma floating in the air. Tea transitions afford us the opportunity to become adaptable, flexible toward ourselves and the world.

Communion with Tea

Tea is to Buddhism as wine is to Holy Communion. In the ritual of Holy Communion, believers drink wine in order to experience and merge with Christ-consciousness. In Buddhism, tea is the drink that best embodies the meditative journey toward spiritual well-being, engendering wakefulness—hence the historical saying, "The taste of tea and Buddhism are one."

Both tea and Buddhism allow us to commune with ourselves, forming a union between who we really are and the world we live in. Our hearts open to the inner truth of our nature in all its simple radiance. We drink in the Buddha within us all. Take some time to meditate on this possibility while you enjoy your next cup of tea.

Mindfulness Meditation:
A Preparation for Appreciating Tea

The first foundation of mindfulness is the body. In this life, we experience all things through our bodies. Please let your body be your home, a refuge of being. Come home to your body as you mindfully prepare it to drink tea.

As we begin to close our eyes, we bring our attention into our body. As your attention moves inward, notice what you sense and feel. Take time to slow down and explore what is present in this moment. Notice where the sensations are occurring and where your attention is drawn. Take a moment as each sensation makes itself known to you to pause and be there for it. Allow the sensations to move freely throughout your body, and realize that you are now in touch with life moving through you. Give some attention to your posture, and let your back be upright without any rigidity, your buttocks solid on the cushion, and your jaw relaxed.

Allow this awareness to include your breathing, and feel the surge of life move through you. Wherever the breath presents itself becomes your point of focus; allow the breath to be just as it is without striving to breathe in a particular fashion. Find this breath at your nostrils, in your chest, or in your abdomen. Sit with the gentle sensations of each breath in each moment, especially noticing the relaxation of the out-breath. The breath may be long or short, smooth or uneven; it makes no difference. Simply take time to feel this aliveness and enjoy whatever sensations come or go. As you sit quietly, focusing within, many thoughts will come and go; simply let them pass like the clouds in the sky. Do not be bothered by thoughts or anything else. Rest in the present moment.

After several minutes, begin to notice how you are feeling. What is the meditation's effect on you? Now you are ready to transition from your meditation. Begin to slowly awaken your body without rushing, moving and stretching each body part. Take the energy, calm, and clarity with you as you go to make your cup of tea.

Guided Meditation on Sensitivity to Prepare for Drinking Tea

Tea drinking is about engaging the senses, recognizing their presence, allowing them to heighten, and becoming aware of how they affect us. When we slow down and prepare to drink tea, we enter the here and now. When we stop our mental chatter, we become highly attuned, our awareness increases, and our sensitivity surfaces. What we didn't notice before, such as the song of the mockingbird, the rustling of the trees in

the wind, children's voices playing on the sidewalk outside, the continual hum of the refrigerator, the water heating in the kettle, the
movement of our bodies, and the breath moving in and out, now occu-
pies our attention. As we become more keenly aware, our senses emerge
from a deep slumber.

The Meditation

Please begin by settling your body. Choose a posture to sit in that is
both comfortable and upright. You may choose to sit in a chair with a
straight back that allows your feet to comfortably touch the floor. You
may also choose to sit on the floor, either cross-legged on a cushion or
zazen style, resting on your knees. Once your position is secure, close
your eyes and gently shift your attention to your breathing. Take the
time to simply notice the breath, allowing it to come and go as it will
without attempting to change anything. Maintain a moment-to-
moment focus on the breath, and allow whatever arises to be there.
Become intimate with your breath, watching and mentally noticing how
it can change and become different: fuller, deeper, longer, more subtle or shallow, or even indistinguishable.

As you sink deeper into your breathing, notice the sounds around you
as they enter. Without getting particularly involved in the sounds, listen to their vibrations; feel the pitch, tone, and intensity as the sounds
enter your ears. Continue to breathe, and simply enjoy the sounds.

As you breathe, turn your attention to your body's sensations. These sensations are always coming and going, visiting for a time, then altering their form and sometimes disappearing. As we attune ourselves carefully to the present moment, we become familiar with the shifting of our physical sensations. While you settle further into yourself, notice whether your sensations feel more precise than they did before; you might pay attention to your body's experience of warmth, chill, tingling, cramping, tightness, spaciousness, and even floating. Continue to breathe, and prepare for the partaking of tea.

Choosing an Object of Attention

Slowly get up, and choose an object that can easily fit in the palm of your hands. Come back to a seated position, and close your eyes. Place the object in open hands, and allow it to rest there while you continue to breathe. Allow your hands to awaken to the object. Give yourself permission to become intimate with the object by slowly bringing it to your face. Take your time, and bring it to your nostrils, inhaling its scent. Once you are aware of its aroma, bring it to your lips and feel its distinct texture against your mouth. Register the sensations. Slowly place it on your cheek. Move the object to other parts of your face, and take your time to note the object's individual characteristics. Treat the object with the care and consideration you would enjoy having extended to you.

Bring the object to your ears and listen to its silent sounds. Slowly return the object to the primary focus of your hands, touching it and discerning its shape and texture. When you feel you've completed this exploration, gradually open your eyes, and engage with whatever they are drawn to. Once your eyes are full, close them again, and continue to breathe. Place the object at your side and rest with your experience. Now you are ready to make your tea and truly engage in the experience of drinking it.

Exercising Our Senses

Each of these exercises is designed to open and engage one of the senses through focused exploration of tea. Enjoy this process.

Seeing

Use your eyes to experience the tea and the tea leaves before and after they are brewed.

Preparation: Put some dry tea leaves into a saucer. Now make a cup of tea. Pour it into a clear or white cup. Put the wet tea leaves into another saucer. Sit down with the tea and the two saucers of leaves in front of you. Close your eyes and settle in.

Exploration: When you open your eyes, gaze at the leaves and the tea. Then carefully examine the contents of each saucer and the cup with your eyes. Notice the coloring and the shape of the leaves. Compare their characteristics. Now look at the tea liquor. Notice its color.

Smelling

Use your sense of smell to experience the tea and the tea leaves before and after they are brewed.

Preparation: Put some dry tea leaves into a saucer. Now make a cup of tea. Pour it into a clear or white cup. Put the wet tea leaves into another saucer. Sit down with the tea and the two saucers of leaves in front of you. Close your eyes and settle in.

Exploration: After you open your eyes, pick up each container one at a time. Smell the leaves and the tea liquor. Breathe deeply to inhale the fragrances fully. Go from one to the next, comparing the similarities and differences.

Touching

Play with your tea leaves—it's a great way to experience tea.

Preparation: Put one tablespoon of dry tea leaves in a wide bowl. Steep another tablespoon of leaves in hot water, and put those tea leaves in a separate bowl. Sit down with the two bowls of tea leaves. Close your eyes and settle in.

Exploration: One bowl at a time, play with the leaves with your fingers. Touch, crunch, pull, twist, rub, tear, and have fun. Try it with your eyes closed, too. Be aware of the differences in the tea leaves.

Hearing

A watched pot may never boil, but you can listen to a pot of water come to a boil.

Preparation: For this exercise, you will need a nonwhistling tea kettle. Fill it three-quarters full with cold water, and place over high heat. Stand or sit near it with eyes closed.

Exploration: Listen carefully to the sounds as the water progresses to the boiling point. Listen to it boil for a minute or two, then turn off the heat.

Tasting

Refine your tasting abilities by comparing two cups of tea that differ only in the amount of time they were brewed.

Preparation: Put enough tea leaves for two cups of tea loose in the pot. Add two cups of water at the appropriate temperature. One minute before the usual steeping time, pour one cup of tea into a cup. Two minutes later, pour the second cup of tea into another cup. The two cups of tea will have been prepared identically except for the amount of time that they have brewed. Sit down with the two different cups of tea. Close your eyes and settle in.

Exploration: Sip one tea, wait a moment, then the other. Carefully compare and contrast the differences in the taste of the two teas.

> "This cup of tea in my two hands
> Mindfulness is help uprightly
> My mind and body dwell
> In the very here and now."

THICH NHAT HANH

Ritual and Ceremony

bringing the sacred into everyday life

❦7❦

"The tearoom is the realm of the sacred."

Joseph Campbell

It is Friday night; the sky is just growing dark as the golden sun dips below the horizon. In a dimly lit room, we see a woman's shadow against the glow of the amber-hued walls. Standing beside a long dining table, she extends her arms out, opening them. Her hands lift a soft piece of cloth and place it on her head. A sudden flicker of light guides our eyes to a candle flame. We discern a candelabra at the center of the long table. Solemn, ancient gestures convey a compelling message of sacredness. Hands educated by a timeless wisdom circle her head and cover her eyes. Her lips whisper inaudible words. The candlelight illuminates her face while her mouth forms a smile, expressing love and reverence.

Tonight these simple, meaningful actions are taking place all over the world. They have been performed by countless women for over five thousand years to begin the Jewish Sabbath. The prayers invoke blessings for the food, and to honor the day of rest. Ceremonies and rituals such as these are practiced at all times of day, by different types of people, and in diverse situations.

The Wisdom of Ritual

The ancient sages used ritual as a way to engage the sacred and create balance in life. In a world governed by seemingly unpredictable and mysterious forces, ritual became the means to recognize, honor, and organize an unfathomable universe. It was a prescription for living that elevated mundane, everyday activities into purposeful, harmonious, and consciously chosen actions. Care, patience, and planning became cornerstones of conduct.

All over the world, every culture and religion expresses its spirituality and its sense of what is sacred through its unique rituals. The Native Americans find purification and connection to their source through the sweat; Jewish people, through the cessation of work, blessings for food and wine, and the invocation of God's name on the Sabbath; some Christians, through receiving the sacrament of Communion; the Chinese, through the celebration of the New Year, which includes replacing misdeeds with positive virtues and eating their food before the Kitchen God; and the Japanese, through *chanoyu*.

101

Rituals are our way of bringing the richness of the sacred into our everyday life. "Spirituality need not be grandiose in its ceremonials," writes Thomas Moore in his book *Care of the Soul*. "Indeed, the soul might benefit most when its spiritual life is performed in the context it favors—ordinary daily vernacular life. But spirituality does demand attention, mindfulness, regularity, and devotion. It asks for some small measure of withdrawal from a world set up to ignore soul." Ceremonies we create for ourselves are our way of reclaiming our soul time so that we can be nourished by whatever we hold sacred. Whether we incorporate new activities into our daily routine or convert some of our daily routine into ritual, this practice will welcome the sacred back into our lives. Chances are, life will no longer seem so mundane as we begin to see that there is much more to life in the present moment.

How Do We Find the Time to Make a Cup of Tea?

For many of us, the sacred has been missing from our lives. Because we are so busy, though, we barely notice its absence, except in times of crisis or tragedy, when we are forced to slow down and face ourselves. Sometimes a prolonged illness, relationship breakup, financial loss, or the loss of a loved one prompts us to reflect upon the meaning of our lives. We look for something to sustain us through the difficult times, when our normal defenses and buffers are disarmed and we feel vulnerable. We feel less secure and more unsure. As hard as they are, though, moments of crisis can open the door to what is precious and sacred in life.

In day-to-day life, we guard our hours with a jealous eye. But when we enter ritual time, the pleasing environment and sacred atmosphere alter our frame of mind. In a tea ceremony, the essence of the tea invites us to slow down, take a deep breath, notice and appreciate our surroundings, as a sense of spaciousness pervades our inner and outer worlds.

102

Rituals replace habituation with animation, by enlivening our feeling for life. In our everyday grind, we can forget to take time to pause, breathe, look up, and feel. The sameness of life turns into listlessness and we are muffled in monotony. Rituals rekindle our raison d'etre. The very nature of the way we drink tea in a ceremony awakens our senses. We become present, alert, and we make an energetic connection to life.

Rituals refocus our eyes, expanding our perceptions, and soon we gaze upon what, till now, has remained unseen. While taking a walk, we notice the ground under our feet, and rocks lose their dull gray appearance. Within each stone, distinctly etched by the winds of time, are strands of blues, greens, purples, and reds, each with its own story to tell. A small, circular rock shaped like a snail may remind us of the circularity of life. But without the awareness to distinguish one rock from another, we trivialize the ordinary, paying it very little attention. We look for beauty in grand and striking ways, all the while missing the simple pleasures in life.

When we enact the rites of a tea ritual, whether those of our own design or those prescribed by tradition, we connect to a beauty that exists deeply within and without. This beauty will not fade like the bloom of a short-lived rose; instead, it endures through the passage of time. It is now that we begin to appreciate things for what they are. We taste with a golden palate, hear with perfect pitch, see with the artist's eye, and touch with the hands of the healer.

103

Just as a well-cooked meal provides nutrients for our physical body to replenish, regenerate, heal, and grow, rituals supply the Recommended Daily Allowances of meaning, value, significance, and nourishment for our spiritual body. When we feel sustained, we have energy and our life force is strong and flowing. We are then ready to be productive—not from a place of strain but from a centered, solid base. Depending on how we approach our lives and our work, they can be full of cherished activity that inspires and vitalizes, or they can be a drain on our resources. Creating rituals can make the difference.

The Tradition of *Li*

Have you ever been taken aback by the silence and stillness of a predawn morning? Have you waited there, gazing, speechless, as if looking into pure space itself? As the eastern sky fills with a large and luminous force, you can hardly contain the feelings of grandeur and power stirring in your chest. A light-generating yellow powerhouse of unknown dimension begins its ascent above the horizon. Illuminating everything in its path, the massive ball's light bathes your body in a warming glow. You're touched in a way you have seldom experienced, and a voice from deep inside calls out to you. Resounding with a familiar yet distant ring, it moves you to bow to the ground, to touch your face to the earth, then to raise your arms to the sky and utter words of praise and appreciation. When you're compelled by some inner and outer force to mirror back what you have witnessed and felt, you become an instrument of something greater.

The ancient Chinese masters of wisdom observed the workings of all things within the universe and then formulated the early ritual observances as a way to bring about harmonious relationships between the visible and invisible forces governing the universe, uniting them in a dynamic balance. This they called *li*. A potent distillation of processes designed to unify the personal and universal, *li* was born from love, awe, respect, and the consciousness that awakened when human beings acknowledged the primal powers that shaped all things.

Over time *li* became a code of conduct governing "noble-minded" people in Confucian China. But as the practice of *li* continued, some sages began to feel that these ritual actions were often performed perfunctorily, as obligatory, empty, and mechanical motions designed to appease the "ancestors." There is a significant difference between enacting rituals as a mere formality versus doing them spontaneously, creatively responding to the mood of the moment and the texture of the day. *Li* is authentic action, not based on what might look good to others but on what arises from within. Different philosophical approaches to Taoism have disagreed about the real purpose of *li*. It is not our concern to determine which school of thought is right, but only to learn about the value of ritual from these beautiful and meaningful traditions.

Our *li* arouses a sincere depth of feeling based on a connection to the unknowable, unnamable forces that govern the universe. *Li* engenders a sense of personal responsibility to do things as well as possible just because they need to be done. It is a creed of right action that comes from an inherent love of all existence, and a link with all that has come before and all that comes after, joined to all of life through an invisible bond of reciprocity. We feel guided to take right action from a place of deep moral imperative. When we honor, respect, and appreciate existence itself, we can say: "The actions I take have significance and merit far beyond my individual self and reflect on others close to me, the community I live in, and the larger world." The timeless ceremonies and rituals of tea are based on these deep understandings.

106

The tradition of *li* aligns us to the natural rhythms that shape the universe. When we create rituals for ourselves that have meaning and purpose, we feel connected to these rhythms. Life, then, seems to make more sense, and many of the emotional and spiritual maladies that afflict our modern cultures, such as hopelessness, despondency, despair, and the associated disorders of addiction and violent behavior, can begin to ease.

Steps for Bringing the Sacred into Everyday Life

Taoists respected and honored the tortoise because it would retreat into itself to restore energy. An old Chinese saying sums this up well: "The tortoise is good at nurturing energy so it can survive a century without food." When we take time and space to bring the sacred into everyday life, we restore our energy, create more energy to take on life's challenges, and develop resources to adapt to difficult conditions. We feel better in every way.

Almost any aspect of daily life can be a portal to the sacred when we build an appropriate framework. The making and drinking of tea can be a vehicle for bringing the sacred into daily living. As such, tea becomes our ritual as well as the magic elixir which heightens our awareness, sharpens our senses, and opens the doors of perception to the sacred. The following suggestions can serve as a blueprint for creating a structure to transform our lives.

107

1. Set an Intention

Bringing the sacred into daily living can be a challenging undertaking. Not only must we believe that we can do it, but we also need discipline— but that doesn't mean that we must have a strong affiliation to a church, synagogue, ashram, community, or teacher on a regular basis, nor that we have to devote hours, days, months, and years of life in prayer, meditation, solitude, abstention, self-sacrifice, service, and surrender to taste a morsel of sacred existence. Such expectations could make our task daunting. Can anyone simply bring the sacred into their lives? The answer is yes.

2. Give Yourself Time

It takes time to become familiar with any new endeavor that we embrace. Whether it is learning equations, making fountains, telemark skiing, or preparing a tea ceremony, we can only develop new skills through practice over time. Cultivating a relaxed attitude toward time and being patient with ourselves are part of being successful.

Let's remember that it takes nine months to gestate a human child. If we rush this process, we encounter problems; certain body parts may be underdeveloped or missing. If we allow the natural progression of gestation to proceed to a full-term birth, usually a child comes into the world equipped with everything he or she needs to function optimally. We can apply this lesson to our lives: as it is, life is challenging enough; why put ourselves at a disadvantage by artificially hastening a natural cycle? There are reasons why things take as long as they do; respecting these processes leads us to a higher quality of life, personal integrity, and optimum health.

3. Cultivate Acceptance and Nonjudgment

When it comes to bringing sacredness into life, most of us are novices. We may feel unsure and unaware of how to establish a sacred reality.

Self-judgment may inhibit us and prevent us from acting; in the worst case, it can paralyze us altogether. But if we embrace the knowledge that we all have "Buddha nature"—meaning that, inside of us, we have a natural goodness and concern for ourselves and all of life—our self-doubt lessens. As we discover this sacredness within ourselves, an innate confidence surges to the forefront of our being.

Acceptance in this case asks us to place attention on the effort, energy, and enthusiasm that we have gleaned from promoting the sacred. Enjoying each step of the process without judging ourselves is fundamental. Doing the best we can do, making a pact with ourselves to adjust our response to whatever needs to be done, is all we can ask of ourselves. If we analyze the actual results of our labors, we turn ourselves into commodities, when if fact we are always in process—dynamic, evolving beings who can create the sacred in everyday life.

109

℘ Setting Your Intention through Ritual Tea Practice

1. Take some time to set an **intention** about what kind of experience you would like to have during this ritual, and what this ritual will help you create or do in your life. The process of reflecting upon ritual time is in itself a ritual.

2. Create a separate **time** from the rest of life that is designated for the sacred. During this time, let others around you know

that you are occupied and would prefer to not be disturbed. Turn off phone machines, faxes, computers, and anything that would interfere with your sacred time.

3. Arrange a **space** that is set up for the sacred. Try to choose a space that will not be disturbed and that you can leave the way you want it. It can be a small—for example, a part of a room that has a screen around it separating it from the rest of the room.

4. Choose a **tea** and aesthetics such as music, flowers, incense, art, and sacred objects that will enhance your enjoyment and help you attain your intention.

5. Center yourself: **breathe**, slow down, and get in touch with yourself. Take time to settle in.

110

Initiation by Ritual

When we participate in a ritual, we experience an integration of breath and space, frequency and vibration, stillness and movement. A carefully choreographed art form, a tea ritual is an all-encompassing, undulating, dance-like movement that surrounds, surrenders, and releases. It expresses the cyclic process of life. Like a wave, continually arriving, briefly staying, and ceaselessly departing, tea ceremony teaches us to embrace whatever the moment presents and graciously let it go, while knowing that it can return over and over again.

✑ Sacred Questions

To help bring ritual into our lives, we can ask ourselves these
    questions:

1. What is my experience and definition of what is sacred? How
   much of a role does it play in my life now? In what ways do I
   already bring the sacred into my everyday life? Do I feel that
   I want more?

2. What areas of my life could be enhanced and enriched by
   incorporating ritual into them (thereby nourishing me
   more)?

3. How often do I take the time to slow down to sense and feel
   what I am doing? Do I take time to notice the beauty in the
   small things in my life?

4. How would it feel to create my own rituals and ceremonies
   and what would they look like? What kind of experience do I
   want to make for myself?

The Tea Ceremony's Mystique

In a tea ceremony, all comes alive. It is the intersection of meditation,
movement, and art. When we enter a space designated for tea, the magic
of the tea muse enters us, and soon, without any prior training, we

reenact the behaviors of a noble lineage of tea practitioners. We don the symbolic robe infused with the knowledge of a transcendent state. In this atmosphere, we can become part of the tea mystique and be more than we ever dreamed we were—exquisitely poised and possessed of fluid motion. A tea ritual broadens our horizons, stretches our minds, extends our limits, and strengthens our capacities.

⟡ What the Tea Ceremony Is

· Breathing consciously

· Watching the tea being poured

· Listening to the tea being poured

· Smelling the aroma of the tea

· Gazing at the meandering steam

· Absorbing the heat of the cup in our hands

· Sensing the warmth of the steam as we drink from the cup

· Tasting the tea in our mouth

" Our whole life could be a ritual; we could learn to stop when the sun goes down and when the sun comes up. We could learn to listen to the wind; we could learn to notice that it's raining or snowing or hailing or calm. . . . If we can hold it all in our hearts, then we can make a proper cup of tea. "

PEMA CHODRON

SHARING TEA
the essence of hospitality

"... Give those with whom you find yourself
every consideration."

SEN NO RIKYU

Showing sincere friendliness, generosity, and consideration for all who enter our world is the hospitality of tea. The word "hospitality" derives from the same root word as "hospital," originally a place of shelter and rest for travelers. Whether we offer tea to a weary traveler or invite a guest to a fancy tea party, the act of opening our hearts and homes to another touches the essence of our humanness. The sharing of tea provides nourishment, creates comfort, and puts all at ease.

The custom of serving tea to our guests is nearly as old as recorded history, a vital part of the tradition of sharing who we are. The earliest reference to tea offered by a host to an honored guest comes to us from the Taoists of China. Around 500 BC, during the Chou Dynasty in China, corruption and folly were bringing about the collapse of the kingdom. According to legend, there lived at this time Lao Tse, a man not only of high rank, but of great wisdom, a true sage. Having no wish to witness the decline of civilization, Lao Tse decided to take his leave from the peopled world. He intended to go to the mountains and live out his days there as a hermit. Heading west, he traveled through the Han Pass, where a gatekeeper named Yin Hsi resided. Legend recounts that Yin Hsi, a sage in his own right, had been waiting for many years in his grass hut at the pass, anticipating that one day an Immortal such as Lao Tse would come this way. In order to entice the master to tarry long enough to share his wisdom, the gatekeeper ceremoniously served Lao Tse a cup of tea. Thus, the well-loved and highly revered Taoist classic the *Tao-te-Ching*, also known as "The Way of Life," was born, transmitted over a cup (or two) of tea. This was the auspicious birth of tea's role in hospitality.

Hospitality Is Connecting with Others

When we gather together with others in the making and serving of tea, something essential happens. Our thoughts gravitate toward our guests' welfare: What do they need? What mood and ambience will bring them satisfaction and happiness? What tea will be most pleasing? How can I help them be most at ease?

In this process we can feel united to others, connected through the time shared over tea. In the company of our guests, we learn all that we hold in common, and we may experience a deep empathy for all of life. Through hospitality, it's possible to know the wisdom in the old saying "It is better to give than to receive."

Opening the Heart

Around the world from ancient to modern times, the way tea is served to others has demonstrated the spirit of hospitality. Although it would be lovely to write about all the tea traditions in the world, our discussion will be limited to the few that have especially touched our hearts and minds.

117

The practice of sharing tea with others is the essence of the Japanese tea ceremony, *chanoyu*. The ceremony is an enactment of "right relationship" to another in a social setting. In the role of the host or hostess, we learn a way of being that celebrates care, precision, and regard toward the well-being of others, the particular situation, and the environment. We bring mindful attention to every person, place, and thing we encounter. As we consider another's needs, our attitude shifts from self to other. As we whisk the tea and present the bowl, our body follows suit, and the peacefulness of serving tea to others infuses our being.

Sen Soshitsu, fifteenth Grand Master of the Urasenke School of Tea, knew that it was "the free and magnanimous heart that counts" in the serving and drinking of tea. It is this caring and considerate, yet tempered and moderated way of being that constitutes the demeanor of the host or hostess at a tea gathering. We serve others without servicing; we offer, without artifice; and we regulate, without controlling.

Consider this lesson in tea etiquette: once a grower invited Sen no Rikyu, the founder of the Japanese Way of Tea, to have tea. He was overjoyed at Rikyu's acceptance, and when Rikyu came for tea, the grower led him into the tearoom and served Rikyu tea himself. However, in his excitement, his hand trembled, he dropped the tea scoop, and he knocked the tea whisk over. The other guests, students of Rikyu, snickered at the tea grower's performance, but Rikyu said, "It was the finest."

On the way home, one of the students asked Rikyu, "Why were you so impressed by such a shameful performance?" Rikyu replied, "This man did not invite me with the idea of showing off his skill. He simply wanted to serve me tea with his whole heart. He devoted himself to completely making a bowl of tea for me, not worrying about errors. I was struck by that sincerity."

Communication through Tea: Etiquette

In the tearoom (*sukiya*), our behavior changes. The protocols of host and guest engage our senses and open our heart, moment by moment. The effects of formal bowing, the aroma of incense, the sounds of simmering water, the intense green of the Matcha tea, and its grassy, bittersweet taste conspire with the appropriately slow pace of the conversation. Drawn in, we engage with others in a new way.

This is called etiquette. It is not simply correct decorum, but a radically different way of relating to each other and our world. Through respectful bowing and periods of silence, the guests waiting for the host to make tea and the host waiting for the guests to drink it, we experience the uniqueness of each living and nonliving thing and recognize its unspoken contribution to the world. The silence is telling. In the absence of regular speech, we begin to taste the flavor of what has been called equanimity, balanced living. And in this state we discover a deeper neutrality, our ability to accept each person for who he or she is and embrace all people as they are.

In the tearoom, time is eternal and space is expansive yet contained. In this receptive and relaxed environment, ordinary constraints and artificial barriers between ourselves and others begin to dissolve. Our everyday thinking patterns become transparent, freeing us to see clearly our automatic behaviors and to relate to others in a truly open way, without judgment and with acceptance.

And we in the tearoom are ennobled, becoming all that we can be. We delight in taking time, allowing others to speak completely, listening to them with enthusiasm and attention, seeing behind our superficial "first impressions," rejoicing in our similarities, and delighting in our differences. In the tearoom, we are filled with a sense of true reciprocity.

Hospitality around the World

When we sip tea, it's a taste of culture in a teacup, a nonverbal experience of ritual custom. Certain cultures view every guest, whether invited or just "dropping by," as a divine messenger, and strangers are welcomed and honored in auspicious ways. For example, the practice of breaking away from whatever one is doing to offer tea to a guest is an important part of British "civility."

The Chinese Tea House

In every part of the world, the teahouse is a public place of hospitality. It signifies a gathering place away from home, where all can come to receive refreshment without discrimination. To the Chinese, a bowl of tea has always been a sign of welcome, whether served in the privacy of one's home or amid the chatter of the teahouse. The first teahouses evolved during tea's golden era, the Tang Dynasty, when tea was served mainly to the upper classes and tea connoisseurs. It was later, during the Qing Dynasty (1644–1911), that we saw the advent of the modern-day teahouse as a social gathering spot for people from all walks of life. The teahouse soon became a regional center where peddlers and farmers could go to for drinks after long hours of selling their wares at the market. A place where business of all kinds was conducted, the teahouse also became a center for town meetings, with impromptu mediators called upon to settle differences. This became such a common practice that the phrase *shang chaguanr*, "to go to the teahouse," also meant to take a dispute to be settled.

The Chinese custom of going to the teahouse has been popular for more than two hundred fifty years (except for a short break during the Cultural Revolution, when the government frowned upon teahouses). The Chinese teahouse of old could be open-air or enclosed, large or small, elegantly decorated or sparsely furnished, with or without music, storytellers, and food. Still places of refuge today, modern teahouses offer both food and drink, and the tradition of dim sum (in which tea is consumed with great assortments of steamed buns) is a favorite pastime. Whether the site of a Gung Fu Tea Ritual or just a spot where those weary from a day of hard work can rest, the teahouse remains a centerpiece in the daily life of the contemporary Chinese person.

The *Chaikhana*, an Afghanistan Teahouse

Can you picture the old Silk Road and a long procession of colorful blankets, carpets, tapestries, and tents draped over slowly moving lines of Arabian horses and slant-eyed camels? This teeming bazaar, which displayed the folk art of Central Asia, spawned a new form of teahouse, the *chaikhana*. A perfect oasis for a weary traveler to rest and have tea!

122

Afghanistan was once the hub of trade along the famous Silk Road. Merchants, traders, artisans, craftsmen, and pilgrims lined the road's cities and marketplaces, where they drank tea, Afghanistan's national beverage, outdoors. The travelers consumed vast quantities of green tea to quench their thirst from the hot, dry desert sun.

When people enter the *chaikhana* today, they remove their shoes before going to sit on the mats that are spread out on brightly colored, hand-woven rugs. An exuberance fills the air and invites us in as we hear the buzz of patrons' voices and the haunting tones of melodious flutes and stringed instruments. Exquisite floral paintings and Persian calligraphy decorate the walls, forming seemingly endless and intricate patterns. The aroma of tea is everywhere as the hot drink is brought forth in round teapots.

A Modern American *Chaikhana*

An homage to the traditional Central Asian teahouse, the Boulder Dushanbe Teahouse in Boulder, Colorado, is available for all to enjoy. The teahouse sits adjacent to the fast-moving, cascading waters of Boulder creek, across from a matrix of green and luxuriant parks. The teahouse is a monument to Persian-inspired art, and the elegantly crafted exterior walls display brightly colored mosaic motifs, each with a decorative floral pattern. The entrance is graced by steps that lead to porticos and patios where one can sit at tables and benches for hours overlooking the creek, park, and foliage.

123

When you walk inside, prepare to enter another realm. Intricate, hand-painted mandalas adorn the ceiling and draw your eyes up. Hand-carved tables, stools, columns, sculptures, and ceramic panels fill the room, gifts from Boulder's sister city, Dushanbe, Tajikistan, where forty artisans contributed their expertise to make this possible. This atmosphere offers an opportunity to feel part of a historic cultural and folk tradition. Here, in a modern city, one can partake of high-quality teas from around the world while being bathed in rare architectural radiance. In our modern life, teahouses like these allow us to experience a home away from home and be served tea in a convivial atmosphere.

Creating the Spirit of Hospitality with Tea

Whether you carefully plan a tea gathering for one guest or several, or welcome a friend for a spur-of-the-moment tea visit, learning to be a gracious host or hostess is key to creating an aura of hospitality. In order to make your tea-time visit a meaningful occasion that you and your guest will both enjoy and prosper from, there are some common tea themes that can be incorporated in your shared time together.

Consideration of Others

Take the time to give thoughtful attention to your guests' favorite and preferred teas, foods, and environments.

Create tea events to celebrate a special time in your guests' life, such as a rite of passage, a birthday, a new job or promotion, or a going-away party. Design the event with them in mind. Ask yourself: What are their needs? Would it be best to make it a quiet, contemplative atmosphere or a social and exuberant experience or a combination of both?

During the tea together, remember to remain mindful of their needs by watching how they are doing: Do they seem at ease, comfortable, engaged, and enjoying themselves? It is important to adjust the particulars of the situation to best serve the guests.

Praise of Others

Before getting together, think about whom you have invited over for tea. Take the time during the tea get-together to convey to others how you appreciate them. This can include sharing what you feel is special about them. You can communicate this appreciation verbally, through the written word, or through some action you take. When you know the other people well, you can let them know how you respect them, how you have learned something from them, and how they may have helped you or someone else.

125

Transforming a Stranger into a Friend

Inviting someone whom you do not know very well over for tea, or asking her to join you in a teahouse, is a way to get to know her better. The person you invite could be an acquaintance from work, a colleague in a similar field, another member of a special interest group you belong to, or someone you have a romantic interest in. The intention, in this time together, is to allow the boundaries of separateness to dissolve and to discover what you share in common.

During this time tell the other person why you wanted to get to know him. Express a sincere interest in him by inquiring about his well-being in all aspects of his life, by exploring his interests, and by listening attentively to his responses.

Unexpected Guests as Divine Messengers

An ancient belief holds that everyone comes into our life for a reason. With that in mind, be spontaneous and open to the company of drop-in visitors by offering whatever tea and food you have. Be willing to discover how and why these unexpected guests have graced your life at this time. What is it that they bring to you, and you to them?

Tea as a Door Opener

You can lessen social awkwardness, which will help others feel at ease and relaxed, by taking the focus off them and placing it on the tea. While serving tea, inform your guests why you chose the particular tea for them, what kind it is, where you purchased it, and what properties and benefits it has. You can also share your thoughts on the tea ware.

Stopping and Enjoying Another's Company

On the spur of the moment, ask a friend if she would like to drop over and do nothing except drink tea and hang out. This implies a readiness to drop other things in favor of getting together with others you don't see often.

Discussing Business and Resolving Differences

Suggest meeting at a teahouse in a neutral atmosphere. This is conducive to brainstorming and exchanging ideas. The teahouse acts as a home away from home in an environment that places the participants on an equal footing. Its relaxing atmosphere also helps to soften what is sometimes hard business.

If you're having conflicts with someone, meeting in the teahouse can support you in joining together cordially, and help you settle any differences.

"I learned to take delight in the pleasure afforded
by a cup of tea. . . . A simple cup of tea has often
been the only spark needed to make an acquaintance, inaugurating a bond of friendship that
could last a lifetime."

P. BRUNETON
En Solitaire Dans L' Himalaya

" In my hands I hold a bowl of tea: I see all of
nature represented in its green color. Closing
my eyes, I found green mountains and pure
water within my own heart. Silently sitting
alone and drinking my tea, I feel these become
part of me. Sharing this bowl of tea with others, they, too, become one with it and nature.
That we can find a lasting tranquility in our
own selves in company with each other is the
paradox that is The Way of Tea."

SEN SOSHITSU XV

129

Since its beginning, the taking of tea has reflected the natural world. Tea drinking, like immersing ourselves in nature, heightens our sensitivity, slows us down, and fosters an appreciation of all things—perhaps that explains why many cultures of the world have brought people and nature together in their tea rituals.

Nature balances the everyday stresses and strains that challenge us in contemporary life. When we sip tea out-of-doors, breathing fresh air in and out, we are cultivating a sustained spiritual ecology.

The Taste of Tea and Nature Are One

Fine teas come from handpicked tea leaves that include only the newest growth: two leaves and a bud. This makes drinking a cup of fine tea an extraordinary experience. Those tea leaves lived a short but vibrant life, only ten days at the most. As we drink the tea from our cup, we are savoring the essence of ten days spent absorbing nature. We are tasting the rise and fall of the temperature as days rolled into nights rolled into days, the finite amount of sunshine and moonshine that showered the leaves, and maybe even some moisture from misty mornings. And we taste the wind. Tea growers say that the amount and type of wind in those ten days have a great deal of influence on the taste of the tea in our cups. The ephemeral essence of nature leaves some record of itself in the tea leaf and offers us a taste of the natural world. With the flavor of rain and wind and sunshine already on our tongues, we can easily begin to smell and see and feel the impressions around us.

Our senses open us to all of life's stimuli, which are continuously touching us in some way. If something "makes an impression on us," as the saying goes, it compels us to stop, notice, and think twice. In a natural environment, the sensory details make a lasting impression because they don't have to compete with overstimulating sound, sight, smell, taste, and touch pollution. We can perceive everything more clearly, such as the sight of the yellow finch making her nest, the scent of the lilac bushes coming into full bloom, the sound of water in the flowing stream, the taste of the tea arising on our breath, and the touch of the breeze on our skin.

131

Tea drinking harmonizes impressions. You can literally drink them in. One of nature's foods, the tea plant grows from the ground like a vegetable. The color of the brew reflects the color of the plant, always a green, yellow, or amber hue. James Norwood Pratt calls tea a "miracle of vegetation." By drinking it, you can feel closer to nature, and a kinship grows.

Nature Yields Us Answers

Nature speaks to us without words. She yields answers to both our voiced and unvoiced questions. Observing her workings, we learn about life cycles, natural processes, death and rebirth, and the balance of forces in our universe. We are a microcosm of her, and she is a mirror of us. If we come to her as a student, needing or wanting direction, she will respond.

When we sit down in a natural environment, a cup of tea helps us to settle in and makes us comfortable. We awaken to the world of sensory impressions around us and drink them in. With each sip, we become more grounded and open to an inner knowing. The tea helps us quiet our mind, come into focus, and find a still point of concentration. We begin to notice if there is something that is longing for our attention, that we wish to come to terms with, or that we want to know more about. Is there an unanswered question nudging at us? With a cup of tea at hand, in a spacious, natural setting, there's room for all of our questions and concerns. Quiet and slow, attuned to every move, breath, and sound, we can receive guidance from nature, that deep source of knowledge that can reflect back to us what we already know, or show us a new way.

Receiving Impressions

The natural world is brimming with bountiful impressions that hover about us like hummingbirds, vibrating at a pitch higher than our normal rate of perception. But we can take them in by simply opening our attention to them.

Just as food sustains our body, impressions are spiritual nourishment that feeds our soul. How do we go about receiving this marvelous food? We begin by noticing that there's another realm apart from our daily experience, a realm that's more subtle and yet more profound.

We can also liken impressions to the "jewel in the lotus," a traditional Buddhist symbol of wholeness and fulfillment. This jewel is available both within us and around us, and we can grasp it by bringing awareness to what is already here. When we are unaware, distracted, or oblivious, caught up in our busy lives, we fail to prosper from this bounty of life. May we all discover this "jewel" and drink it in!

Just as the Buddhist monks used tea to help them keep the mind alert, eyes open, and body relaxed during sitting meditation, tea can enhance our efforts to appreciate the natural wonders around us. It can amplify our stillness so that we become attuned to the stillness around us. Many of the skills we have developed in the minutes and hours spent drinking our daily tea—being still, taking time for being, creating a sacred space, maintaining an alert wakefulness, and tuning in with a keen sensitivity—are the very qualities we need to enter an intimate communion with nature. When we have the opportunity to find a special spot in nature where we can retreat, its beauty can inspire us to appreciate the impressions that are offered in abundance.

133

The Poetry of Tea

The natural world can be a place to find answers, make decisions, and deal with major life events. Time spent out in nature restores our equilibrium. Moses went to Mt. Sinai to receive guidance, Jesus retreated to the wilderness, and Buddha sat under to the Bodhi tree to gain his enlightenment. The early tea sages sought solitude and refuge amid the mountains of ancient China in order to live close to nature and her teachings. Here, they postulated a tea wisdom, a philosophy of harmonious living that reflected the relationships among the natural forces that govern our world. They composed inspired and ecstatic prose and poetry, with their words evoking the mist on the mountains and the forests where tea grows. These images allow us to taste the tea and feel the air, as if we were there. They stir the cauldron of our thoughts, churning up feelings that dwell below the surface.

> "Emerald trees on Lushan
>
> Are held in swirling mist.
>
> No wine can touch the senses
>
> Like this tea made with spring water."

BAI JUYI, TANG DYNASTY POET

The subtle undertones of Japanese verse can touch us unexpectedly. Through these poems, we experience tinges of life's impermanence.

> "In the old cave Spring comes
>
> And I am looking at the azure bay,
>
> While steam rises from the boiling tea,
>
> The evening deepens, and the air is a quiet cloud."

UNKNOWN POET FROM THE RYOUNSHU ANTHOLOGY

Tea poetry is infused with the spirit of nature. The deep respect and abiding love the tea votaries had for nature has suffused their every word. The first tea teachers were ancient sages who observed all the phenomena under heaven and whose teachings included ritualized observances to maintain a balance between the forces of nature and man. When we read poetry and drink tea, we can actually sense ourselves in alignment with these very forces.

135

Musing over Tea

The word "musing" comes from a Greek word that means "to play." In Greek lore, the Muses were the initiators of music, poetry, song, and dance that inspired others to participate. When we activate the muse, we allow our imagination to soar and our mind to speculate and inquire. Musing is a free-ranging movement of the mind, feelings, and spirit. Through musing, we let go of preconceived thoughts and empty ourselves to an expanse of ecstatic feeling. Musing is an open-ended exploration of our possibilities. It is a personal stream of consciousness that allows what is below the surface to rise, flow, and emerge.

Drinking tea helps to free the muse in us. When we drink tea, our spirits rise, our senses sharpen, and we perceive the world with heightened clarity. The tea simultaneously focuses us and encourages our thoughts to roam freely, mingling with inspired feelings. When we drink tea and muse out of doors, we can fully experience the richness of the natural world. Tea, combined with the splendor of nature, loosens our mind and releases our inherent creativity.

Tea Gardens

Designing gardens based on the carefully observed laws of nature was a centuries-old tradition in Japan even at the time of Sen no Rikyu. A diversity of styles developed over time, such as the mainly Shinto practice of building shrines sanctifying spaces dedicated to the spirits housed in hills, trees, and stones; the formal Chinese gardens that replicated cosmological order; the stark and abstract meditation gardens of the monasteries; and the relaxed art of strolling gardens whose designs attempted to recreate the paradise-to-come of Pure Land Buddhism. All were based on the idea that retreating to the natural beauty of the garden to find refuge from worldly involvement, if only temporarily, was heaven to the soul.

Later, when tea gardens were created as a setting for the tea hut, Sen no Rikyu's aesthetic of impoverished elegance influenced designs. These gardens contain nothing lavish such as brilliant beds of flowers or ornate statues, but whenever possible, they will include modest glimpses of noteworthy natural features beyond the boundary of the garden itself. The tea garden features stone paths that lead us from the mundane world to another world—physically, mentally, and spiritually, by guiding us through the gates, to the basin, and around the bend to the tea hut.

137

In the Roji

Passing through the outer gate of the tea garden, we enter the outer *roji*, where we find a place to adjust our clothing and ready ourselves. We then proceed to the waiting bench, where we take our seats, sit quietly, and mentally prepare ourselves for the transition to the inner *roji*. The sight and sound of the host filling a stone basin, the *tsukubai*, with fresh spring water signals the beginning of the tea ceremony. After symbolically purifying himself at the *tsukubai*, the host opens the middle gate and bows in greeting, welcoming us to the inner *roji*.

Each of us in turn follows the path and enters through the second or middle gate. Though the gate itself is never elaborate or heavy, its symbolic significance is great. Stepping through this gate and closing it behind us, we reach a turning point in the path. We step into another world, where nature's spirit creates for us a place to seek refuge from the mundane, a place to find spiritual renewal. The stepping stones we follow have been moistened. The impression of dew-kissed rocks and moss at our feet imparts a feeling of purity and undisturbed tranquility. Without words, the moisture speaks of the Buddhist teachings in the Parables of the Lotus Sutra: the dewy ground is where we sit when we are liberated from the consuming passions of the world.

We approach the *tsukubai*, kneel, and take the bamboo ladle. We wash one hand, then the other, and rinse our mouth with the fresh water, a ritual that cleanses body, mind, and soul. Some consider this to be the critical moment, when we wash away everything that distracts and impedes, and make ourselves ready to experience the feelings of harmony, purity, respect, and tranquility that *chanoyu* promises. Proceeding slowly, we gaze upon every element of the garden, the rocks, moss, leaves, and wood, and their artful arrangement. In the heart of the garden, nature and her elements provide a sanctuary for the teahouse, the ideal environment for appreciating beauty and sharing a bowl of tea with heartfelt sincerity.

Opening the Gate to Our Own Inner *Roji*

Walking the path of the *roji* represents the journey we make when we seek that place of peace and tranquility within ourselves through communion in nature. As at the first gate, we extricate ourselves from our daily routine, change our clothes, and get together whatever else we need for wherever we are going, whether it's a garden in the backyard, a neighborhood park, or nearby woods. Arriving, it's a good idea to just sit for a moment to give ourselves time to attune to the surroundings. We may have come with an idea of where to sit or which path to take, but pausing, we may find ourselves lured to go in another direction. Stepping through "the middle gate" (metaphorically speaking), we enter the inner sanctuary, closer to nature and ourselves. As we are drawn deeper into the woods or garden or park, and into the natural world around us, we are moved toward a more inner experience of our selves. Finding a spot, we sit, gather concentration, and prepare our tea. While sipping tea, we let the hot brew dissolve the previous concerns of the day and bring us into focus in the here and now. As we gaze around us, attuning ourselves to the sights, sounds, smells, and feeling of our environment, we can rest in our own true nature.

139

Setting Yourself Up for an Outdoor Tea Ritual

When you're planning an outdoor tea ritual, please allow inspiration to move through you and the tea itself. Prepare for the unexpected, and give serendipity and spontaneity a chance to express themselves.

Find a spot that is nurturing and comfortable and can afford you an open view of the mountains, valleys, fields, trees, plants, or water. The edge of an open meadow could be an ideal place. Be sure there's enough flat ground in front of the area where you sit to make the tea.

Spread out your blanket or other ground cover, sit down, and set your belongings and tea equipment to the side. Take a few quiet minutes to breathe and center yourself; meditate if you are moved to do so.

When you feel ready, carefully assemble the tea ware you need. Make the tea. Next, clear the space in front of you by setting everything aside but the teacup, teapot, and warmer.

Take a few minutes to close your eyes, settle in, and breathe.

Open your eyes when you feel ready and let them rest comfortably on some object in the environment like a tree, plant, flower, or rock, with a gentle, soft focus.

Slowly lift the teacup, feeling the warmth, the texture, and the fit of the cup in your hands. Bring it to your nostrils and breathe in the aroma; put it in front of you and gaze at the color; raise it to your lips and begin to taste the tea. Notice, and give yourself a moment to appreciate and enjoy. After one or two sips, set the teacup down.

Now you can look around at your nearby environment with relaxed eyes. Allow your focus to expand to take in the larger panorama. With a receptive mind and spirit, let the sights, sounds, smells, tastes, and touches of the natural world impress you.

Continue sipping the tea with a relaxed and mindful presence. Give your attention the opportunity to float freely between drinking the tea and absorbing the impressions.

If a desire to move arises when you finish the tea, feel free to take a walk. Move slowly, without rushing, so that you won't disrupt any beneficial effects you might have experienced from sitting with tea and nature. You may notice a subtle shift in energy or a more profound state of heightened awareness.

141

Please enjoy and be happy!

Taking Tea Outdoors

For making tea outdoors, you will need to bring with you:

- · Water
- · A small portable gas stove

- Matches
- A windscreen (optional)
- A small pot for boiling water
- A teapot or container for brewing tea
- Tea leaves
- Tea strainer
- Cup for drinking
- Tea warmer with tea light (optional)

Enhancing Our Lives through Tea

Tea has enhanced our own lives in many ways. It has refined our way of moving, teaching us to carry ourselves with grace, dignity, and precision—helping us to develop a newfound sense of our bodies. We tread gently, aware of our personal impact upon the world and respectful of all that we encounter along the way. Learning to make tea becomes an exquisite and personal art.

It's also a way of being and doing that can inform our entire lifestyle. It allows us to do whatever we do well, take time to pause and reflect, and contemplate our actions deeply. Tea does not tell us what to do, or what to reflect on, or what actions to take. It only encourages us to pursue our endeavors mindfully, thoughtfully, with integrity and consideration—all the qualities that we learned through making a cup of tea well apply to doing anything well. The spirit of tea invokes a sense of caring and attention, a feeling for excellence that can have a positive influence in every part of our lives.

> "In conclusion, let me say to you that whatever nation and culture you come from, and whatever traditions you embrace, I hope that your journey in life will be filled with joy. But no matter how or where you follow your path, don't forget to take the tea!"

BROTHER JOSEPH KEENAN   143

How to Learn More about Tea

There are four ways to learn about tea:

1. Drink a lot of tea, with awareness and openness to truly taste and experience it.

2. Drink a lot of tea with others, and share experiences and observations, learning from each other. One good place to do this is at the teahouse; later in this section, we offer a short list of some of the teahouses we have been to that offer enjoyable and unique tea experiences.

3. Drink a lot of tea, and travel to places where tea is grown, to experience tea production and the cultures of tea firsthand. There are tea people who lead such tours that can be found on the Web, but because we have not been on a tour, we won't include a recommendation here.

4. Drink a lot of tea, and read about tea. There are many books being written about all aspects of tea, and original Chinese and Japanese texts are being translated into English. Later in this section, we have included a list of the books we have enjoyed and learned from, as well as a few websites where you can find information about the latest studies regarding the health benefits of tea.

Tea Sources

These are some of our favorites; there are more on the Web every time we look.

Bodhidharma Tea Company
www.bodhidharmateacompany.com
303-402-9576

TeaCup
www.seattleteacup.com
2207 Queen Anne Avenue North
Seattle, WA 98109
206-283-5931

Red Crane Teas
303-477-3642

SpecialTeas
www.specialteas.com
888-365-6983

Favorite Teahouses

Chado Tea Room

www.chadotea.com
8422-1/2 West Third Street
Los Angeles, CA 90048
800-442-4019

What makes Chado such a wonderful tea experience is the extensive tea list and how perfectly the tea is brewed and served. Take some time with the tea list; ask for recommendations if you need guidance. Whatever tea you choose will be brought to you fully brewed in a cozy-covered teapot. Many teahouses serve tea, but not that many serve it so well brewed. Chado now has a teahouse in Pasadena. Bulk teas are available as well.

Seven Cups Teahouse

www.sevencups.com
2516 East 6th Street
Tucson, AZ 85716

Decorated in the style of an authentic Chinese teahouse, Seven Cups offers a serene setting in which to appreciate fine, certified organic teas imported from China and around the world. The shop also sells other premium organic teas and specialty tea ware.

The Imperial Tea Court

www.imperialtea.com
1411 Powell Street
San Francisco, CA 94133
800-567-5898

A wonderful Chinese-style teahouse in San Francisco, The Imperial Tea Court has been offering a ceremonial tea service for several years. An exotic environment with helpful service allows you to enjoy drinking tea. And you can purchase both tea and authentic Chinese tea ware to bring home. The Imperial Tea Court has recently opened another teahouse in San Francisco called the Ferry Building Teahouse, which we have not yet visited.

The Tao of Tea

www.taooftea.com
3430 Southeast Belmont Street
Portland, OR 97214
503-736-0198

The Tao of Tea operates three different sites in Portland. At their Belmont street teahouse, you can choose your experience. The teahouse is divided by a hallway. One side is the café, where you can order a light meal or a snack to go with your tea. The other side is the leaves room, where tea is available to buy by the ounce, or you can order a pot from the menu. The quiet ambience here focuses on the tea and encourages reading or subdued conversation. In the back is a

Gung Fu tea bar, where the experienced staff brews up a pot of oolong for you.

At their teahouse at the Portland Classical Chinese Garden, in keeping with tradition, Tao of Tea serves only Chinese teas in Chinese-style tea ware. Pearl District teahouse, a four-and-a-half-mat tearoom for *chanoyu* within the larger store and café. In every store, the taste of tea is enhanced by the experience of tea.

The Boulder Dushanbe Teahouse
www.boulderdushanbeteahouse.com
1770 13th Street
Boulder, CO
303-442-4993

Please refer to the Sharing Tea chapter of *Tea Here Now* to read about this teahouse. Known for enjoyable dining as well as tea drinking, it's well worth visiting.

Recommended Reading

For general information about tea, these are the two books we recommend first:

Pratt, James Norwood. *New Tea Lover's Treasury.* San Francisco: Publishing Technology Associates, 1999.

149

This is one of the best comprehensive sources about tea available today, written by the American statesman for tea. The first half of the book paints a complete and colorful picture of tea's role in world history. In the second half, Pratt describes the many teas of today and where they come from. We can highly recommend it as your first tea book, and we still refer to it often.

Lam, Master Kam Chuen with Lam, Kai Sin and Lam, Tin Yu. *The Way of Tea*. Singapore: Gaia Books Ltd, 2002.

Though this small volume elucidates only aspects of tea in China, it covers some important ground, since China is the ancestral home to tea and tea drinking, as well as the present-day producer of almost 25 percent of the world's tea. Among its color pictures, it includes a step-by-step photo essay with easy-to-follow instructions for Gung Fu Tea and other traditional ways to brew and drink Chinese teas.

For books that focus on the art and culture of tea, we recommend:

Sen, Grand Master Soshitsu. *The Japanese Way of Tea*. Honolulu: University of Hawai'i Press, 1998.

This is the story of tea's origins in China, its immigration to Japan, and the evolution of *chado*, the Japanese Way of Tea, also known as *chanoyu*, the Japanese tea ceremony. It was written by the fifteenth Grand Tea Master of Urasenke who, since writing the book, has retired (his son has stepped up to that position). If you are new to *chanoyu*, read this book first for a comprehensive history. If you want to learn more about the Japanese Way of Tea, we also recommend these books, all by Sen Soshito XV:

Chado. New York and Tokyo: John Weatherhill, Inc., 1979.

Tea Life, Tea Mind. New York and Tokyo: John Weatherhill, Inc., 1985.

The Spirit of Tea. Kyoto: Tankosha, 2003.

These two books talk more about tea as a Buddhist or Zen path:

151

Hammitzsch, Horst. *Zen in the Art of the Tea Ceremony*. New York: St. Martin's Press, 1981.

Hirota, Dennis, ed. *Wind in the Pines.* California: Asian Humanities Press, 1995.

There are two very lovely books about the culture of tea in China:

Blofeld, John. *The Chinese Art of Tea.* Boston: Shambhala, 1985.

Reprinted in recent years, this book was written by a man who loved and appreciated the Chinese, their culture, Taoism, and tea. Through

history and legends, as well as personal experience and scholarly
research done during his twenty years in China, he describes the context in which tea and the appreciation of tea developed.

Ling, Wang. *Chinese Tea Culture*. Beijing: Foreign Language Press, 2000.

You may have to search around for this small English-language book
printed in China, but it is a jewel worth looking for. It's a charming
account of the history of tea and includes chapters with such titles as
"Tea and Social Rites," "Folk Tea Art," and "Tea Customs of Ethnic
Groups of China." It's a refreshingly different and Chinese perspective on the virtues of tea. At one point, the author urges the reader to
cultivate honesty, elegant taste, and an active attitude toward life with
the spirit of tea. How can we say no?

If you are building your own tea library, you would have to include:

Yu, Lu and Carpenter, Francis Ross, trans. *The Classic of Tea*. New
Jersey: The Ecco Press, 1974.

This is a translation of the original treatise by none other than Lu Yu,
the Chinese patron saint of tea. It is a piece of history, and still quot-
ed from, though most of the "practical" instructions for firing and
brewing your own tea are not all that practical anymore. If you get the
translation by Francis Ross Carpenter, her introduction is informa-
tive and interesting.

If you are interested in the British experience of tea and its roots, then we recommend:

Pettigrew, Jane. *A Social History of Tea*. London: National Trust Enterprises, Ltd., 2001.

The British were not the first Europeans to drink tea at home (the Dutch were), but they were perhaps the most enthusiastic. Ever since tea arrived in England around 1660, the British and tea have been inseparable, influencing each other's history, character, and fashions. This book is a lively written account of the British love affair with tea by a British tea expert who travels the world lecturing on many aspects of tea.

153

A Few Websites

In addition to the many merchant websites that offer lots of information about the health benefits of tea, there are health-related websites with reports on the latest studies.

www.nutrition.org
The American Society of Nutritional Sciences offers free abstracts of published research findings from many science and medical journals. Use keyword "tea."

www.teausa.com
The Tea Association and the Tea Council of the USA, as well as the Specialty Tea Institute, have compiled information about the health benefits of tea, with references to research studies.

www.americanheart.org
Search for "tea," and get the latest on heart health news and tea.

www.cancer.org
Search for "tea" to learn the latest on tea and cancer.

ACKNOWLEDGEMENTS

Our Thanks

We are so very fortunate to be working with the people at Inner Ocean Publishing. Their commitment to this book project and their excitement about the manuscript confirmed in us the merit of our efforts. Heather McArthur embraced the spirit of tea in her editing and brought a clear perspective in reorganizing the sequence and pacing of the chapters, with a cup of tea in hand. She has been wonderful to work with. Alma Bune has guided the direction of this process, always available to answer questions and offer help to novice book writers. We thank you both so very much for making the editing process interesting and fun.

We also take this opportunity to acknowledge James Norwood Pratt, tea statesman extraordinaire, whose enthusiasm and knowledge about tea, fortunately, cannot be contained. Through his writings and lectures, he has done much to inspire and educate all of us about the history, romance, and treasury of tea. We thank you for being a friend of tea, and a tea friend.

Lhasha's Acknowledgements

In writing this book, my appreciation goes first and foremost to my husband, Russell Lowes. Russ has consistently afforded me the time and space to "do tea" and write about it. Although not a tea drinker himself, he has always honored and respected my devotion to tea. This is demonstrative of the unconditional love we all hope for.

I am honored and grateful to have a friend and fellow traveler on the path of tea and mindfulness, Wayne Blankenship. Wayne's insightful advice and writing skills in crafting our book proposal to Inner Ocean Publishing helped put this process in motion. His enthusiasm for this project has never waned.

My sincere thankfulness goes to my manager at Miraval Life in Balance, Natasha Korshak, for her good faith in me, for her help in bringing the "Spirit of Tea" classes to Miraval, and for her ongoing support of my teaching. Working at Miraval is a fulfilling experience and the opportunity to be part of the staff with its dedication to "life in balance" has supported this writing endeavor and mindful living. The teachings in mindfulness and meditation by the Spirit Rock meditation teachers, Anna Douglas and Shinzea Young have been priceless—my heartfelt thanks.

I am fortunate to have two wonderful Japanese tea instructors who have patiently offered their time and teaching in my study of *chanoyu,*

Sensei Keiko Nakada in Phoenix and Pasadena and Sakina Von Briesen in Santa Fe. Although I have always had to travel a great distance to study, they have both encouraged my efforts. It is their devotion to teaching that has allowed me to pursue this path of study.

Donna's Acknowledgements

My travels through the world of tea have been enriched by everyone who has shared tea with me, sat beside me as a student in the tea room, and written or spoken about tea. In particular, my journey has been guided and made all the more enjoyable by my tea mentors and good friends, Stephanie Klausner and Brian Keating. Thanks to each of you for generously sharing your considerable knowledge and excellent teas with me over the years.

My deep appreciation for the spirit of tea and its rituals has been fostered by the tradition of *chado*, The Way of Tea. This wellspring of teachings has been made available to me through the understanding, wisdom, and experience of my tea teachers, who have so graciously instructed me. To Bonnie Mitchell and Tim Olson of Urasenke Seattle; Hobart and Carol Bell and Shoshana Cooper, whom I studied with in Boulder; and Sakina Von Briesen of Urasenke New Mexico: *Sensei, okeiko arigato gozaimashita.*

Most of all I thank my husband, Aiy'm, who sits and sips tea most mornings in the Boulder foothills, a tea votary in his own right. His unfaltering encouragement and wholehearted support of my many tea endeavors have been invaluable throughout the process of writing this book. I'm so grateful to have him as co-creator in my tea life.

Donna Fellman is director of the Tea Education Alliance, dedicated to promoting tea and the tea lifestyle through education and experience. She is also owner of the Bodhidharma Tea Company, specializing in tea and tea ware for the contemplative lifestyle. She teaches, lectures, and consults about all aspects of tea. She lives the tea lifestyle in Louisville, Colorado, with her husband, Aiy'm, and their cat, Sencha.

Lhasha Tizer works at Miraval Life in Balance Resort, where she teaches classes and conducts personal consultations about tea, mindfulness, and meditation. She consults, coaches, and instructs others in creating mindful and healthy lifestyles through her business, The Way of Wellness. She educates, as well as creates special tea ceremonies and events for others. She lives peacefully and contentedly in Tucson, Arizona, with her husband, Russell. Lhasha has four grown children and three grandchildren who fill her life with love.

For more information about the authors and the *Tea Here Now* workshops, visit www.TeaHereNow.com

159

A Toast to Tea and Life

In the tea pot something magical happens.
An invisible transformation occurs that alters our mood
    and lifts our spirit.
There is an invitation to become connoisseurs of an art form as
    old as civilization itself.
The ever-evolving world of tea welcomes us as aestheticians of life:
able to mold and shape the texture and temperament of the day.
The adaptable, all-occasion spirit of tea sparks a renewal of
    playfulness and possibility.
With a simple cup of tea in hand we toast to creatively engaging and
    fully responding to our lives.
To tea and life!